Man OVERBOARD:

The Counterfeit Resurrection of Phil Champagne

Man OVERBOARD:

The Counterfeit Resurrection of Phil Champagne

Burl Barer

Northwest Publishing, Inc.
Salt Lake City, Utah

Man Overboard:
The Counterfeit Resurrection of Phil Champagne

For information address: Northwest Publishing, Inc.
6906 South 300 West, Salt Lake City, Utah 84047
SCM 12 13 94
Edited by C. C. Robbins

PRINTING HISTORY
First Printing 1995

ISBN: 1-56901-815-4

NPI books are published by Northwest Publishing, Incorporated,
6906 South 300 West, Salt Lake City, Utah 84047.
The name "NPI" and the "NPI" logo are trademarks belonging to
Northwest Publishing, Incorporated.

PRINTED IN THE UNITED STATES OF AMERICA.
10 9 8 7 6 5 4 3 2 1

Yes, Mom, I'm writing.

Acknowledgments

When someone becomes famous or infamous they relinquish their right to a private life. They become, by nature of their deeds or misdeeds, a public person subject to relentless investigation, evaluation, and interpretation. Such is the case with Phil Champagne.

As all lives are intertwined, to exclude Mr. Champagne's extended family and coterie of friends from the following narrative would be both impossible and impractical. In deference to the wishes of Mr. Champagne's children, no statements made by them to the author are utilized in the text.

This story is admittedly far-fetched, filled with fraud, deception, trickery, lies, illusion, and irrefutable facts. Names and locations revealed under oath, discovered in public records, or documented by law enforcement agencies or insurance investigators have not been changed for anyone's protection or convenience. Certain players and locations in this adventure have been given slightly modified identification, but modified identification runs rampant in this story anyway.

Special thanks to Phil Champagne; Barb Fraley Campagne; Lyle Workman of the United States Secret Service; Assistant U.S. Prosecutor Timothy Ohms; Ed Grass; John Robin Champagne; Peter Richter; Henry kantor; Don Robertson; Richard Sanger; Gary Penar; Richard Fraley, Sr.; Rich Fraley, Jr.; Monte LeHew, Sr.; Agent Tom Sommero of the U.S. Department of Labor; The Police Department of Boca Raton, Florida; Ann Rule; Gary C. King; Lee Goldberg; Phil Krupp; Anthony Spinner; Leonard and Iris Bell; David and Jilla Simmons; Tom and Susan Bartholomew for their kind hospitality; Leslie Stahlhut and Christopher Robbins for their wise editing; to my agent, David Hiatt, for his faith in this project; and to Buck Ormsby for suggesting it in the first place. Thanks to everyone who provided encouragement or shared their time, resources, and memories, especially my wife and kids.

The photo montage entered as an exhibit in the case against Barb Fraley is comprised of photographs from the files of Spokane County. The inclusion of a woman's photograph in the montage does not imply criminal activity by that woman, nor should any such inference be made.

As for Harold Richard Stegeman, may he rest in peace.

One

...but how much adventure is free from all taint of coincidence? Coincidences are always coinciding—it is one of their peculiar attributes; but the adventure is born of what the man makes of his coincidences.

—Leslie Charteris
The Man Who Could Not Die

...and when We deliver him to dry land, then does he compromise.

The Qur'an

Phil Champagne died August 31, 1982, in a tragic boating accident off Lopez Island, Washington. He was fifty-two. Champagne was survived by his wife of twenty-eight years, four grown children, an octogenarian mother, and two despondent brothers. Phil didn't know he was dead until he read it in the paper. All things considered, he took it rather well.

Standing six foot two, 205 pounds, wearing a Ronald Coleman mustache and demeanor to match, Phil Champagne is a well-aged, blue-eyed, Errol Flynn style swashbuckler who appears as if he should be starring in an RKO "Falcon" movie with George Sanders or Tom Conway.

"Don't call me Harold Stegeman." The request is polite, yet firm. There is a mischievous twinkle under the graying brows of the former Harold Stegeman, known to some as Frank Wincheski, known to yet others as Peter Donovan.

"My name is Phil Champagne. I'm pleased to meet you." The debonair and once elusive man extends his hand in greeting. "I was born June 30, 1930, and died in a tragic boating accident in August of '82, in the waters of the Strait of Juan de Fuca."

Prior to the accident, Phil Champagne's adult life had been, in a word, average. In two words, dull and boring. Death—a single splash followed by silence and pursued by searchlights—changed everything.

"There are no words adequate to describe the intoxicating sense of liberation I experienced when I realized I was dead. It was the unexpected answer to an unspoken prayer," admits Champagne, now in his early sixties. "In the first heady rush of what was perhaps trauma-induced delusion, I decided to be the one thing in death that I had never been in life—an adventurer."

The Secret Service and the FBI prefer the term "convicted felon," although Champagne did not spend twenty-one months in a minimum security federal prison for faking his death.

"I didn't fake it," insists Champagne. "I simply didn't contradict it."

Why would a respected Portland, Oregon, businessman with an essentially crime-free adult life, an excellent career, but otherwise lackluster existence, allow his family, friends, and business associates to believe he had drowned in an accidental fall from a sailboat?

"Having lost my life, I had nothing to lose," says Phil. "I figured no one would starve to death if I wasn't around. I was leaving my wife and kids, but she didn't like me anyway, the children were grown..." Phil's voice trails off. "And no matter what Special Agent Goodman thinks, it wasn't an insurance scam."

Neil Goodman, Special Agent in charge of the Secret Service office in Spokane, Washington, went public with his emphatic disagreement shortly after Champagne's controversial incarceration.

"Our investigation has determined that Mr. Champagne apparently faked his own death to facilitate an insurance fraud," Goodman delineated to reporters on May 1, 1992. "At least two policies paid out and there may be others we don't know about at this point. At least two other men, including one of Champagne's brothers, were aboard and presumably were involved in the fraudulent report."

Presumptions are one thing, indictments another. After extensive investigation into the matter by law enforcement agencies, no criminal charges were filed against either Mitch Champagne, Phil's older brother, or John Champagne, his younger brother. Phil Champagne died fair and square.

"Honest to God," insists an exasperated Phil Champagne, "the Secret Service could win the conclusion jumping competition in the Olympics. Just because Mitch had a $1.5 million policy on my life doesn't mean he had anything to do with my death. The policy wasn't his idea in the first place, and it sure as hell wasn't mine."

"Phil is telling the truth," remarks Oregon insurance agent and real estate developer Ed Grass. "I'm the one who suggested that Mitch take out what's called Key Man insurance on Phil."

A personable and gregarious man with a slight build and snappy goatee, Ed was introduced to the enterprising Champagne brothers in the 1970s by Gresham attorney Don Robertson.

"I was anticipating a nice little commission for selling Mitch the insurance," recalls Grass, "but Mitch decided to get the coverage from Federal Kemper with whom he was already doing business."

So it was simply prudent business advice that had convinced Portland real estate developer William M. "Mitch" Champagne to purchase a $1.5 million policy on his brother, Phillip, whom he had hired to oversee his rapidly expanding construction empire.

When Phil Champagne disappeared without a trace into the dark, cold waters off the San Juan Islands, Federal Kemper was understandably reluctant to release the money without a recovered body. Mitch demanded payment from Kemper on November 12, 1982 and filed suit to collect in May 1983. A settlement was reached, and in November 1983, Federal Kemper paid Champagne's company $700,000.

According to court documents "Federal Kemper paid less than the face amount of the policy in the context of substantial uncertainty in the fact of Phillip Champagne's death."

When Phil turned up alive and imprisoned in 1992, the insurance company sued Mitch to recover, claiming a settlement condition required Mitch Champagne to repay the money if his brother was ever found alive. Mitch Champagne resisted the suit on the grounds that a seven-year "enforceability period" had expired before it was filed.

"Mitch Champagne first learned his brother was alive when Federal Kemper served him with a summons for the insurance company's lawsuit," explained his lawyer, Henry Kantor, of Portland. "Mitch's reaction upon learning his brother was alive was absolute astonishment, which soon gave way to anger."

While Federal Kemper would appreciate having the money returned, Kemper's legal representative, Peter Richter, acknowledged that the insurance company made no claim of fraud in its lawsuit against Mitch Champagne.

While Mitch had been devastated by his brother's death, Phil's high-profile resurrection added legal insults to emotional injury.

"Mitch finds this entire situation humiliating and embarrassing," elaborated Mitch's attorney, Henry Kantor. "He lost his brother twice: once when Phil fell overboard and again when he resurfaced as a criminal. After ten years of grieving over the loss of his younger brother, he discovered that he had been deceived. Mitch is a victim of Phil's deception and, as far as I know, the brothers haven't spoken since Phillip turned up alive."

When the unexpected resurrection of Phil Champagne hit the headlines, the mavens of media collided in the halls of justice. Tabloids, talk shows, and first-run syndication television productions pushed the strange case of Phil Champagne to the top of their most-wanted list. Everyone wanted a salable piece of the not-so-dead deceased.

Including his two bereaved daughters.

Kathy and Renee, a Champagne pair of opportunistic offspring, steadfastly refused to grant even the most minimal press interviews. The reason cited for their icy silence was far from their Uncle Mitch's understandable aversion to public humiliation—they wanted money.

Barbara LeHew Fraley, longtime companion of Harold Richard Stegeman of Hayden Lake, Idaho, had never heard of Phil Champagne, his brother Mitch, his daughters Kathy and Renee, or Federal Kemper Life Assurance Company. From October 1987 until debts and overhead put them out of business in 1990, she, Harold, and her five children from a previous marriage had run Barb's Country Kitchen Restaurant along State Route 3 between Shelton and Bremerton, Washington.

On November 6, 1991, Harold, Barb, and her son, Richard, stopped in Ritzville, Washington, for breakfast at Perkins Restaurant. Located sixty miles southwest of Spokane along Interstate 90, Perkins has built its reputation on pancakes. After a pleasant meal, Barb paid for their ticket with a hundred dollar bill Harold had given her.

It was counterfeit.

Dragged from the pancake house in handcuffs, Barb pleaded ignorance. Harold went home to destroy evidence.

He failed.

Four months later, on Thursday, March 12, 1992, a state department investigator obtained a warrant to search the home of Harold Stegeman. While searching Stegeman's briefcase for evidence of Stegeman's true identity, agents found a negative of a seal used on U.S. currency and other evidence linked to counterfeiting. What the State Department had initially been looking for was Stegeman's passport.

They had already determined that a Harold Richard Stegeman had been born at University Hospital in Coral Gables, Florida, on June 20, 1937, to Paul and Marie Stegeman. Paul Raymond Stegeman and the former Marie Elizabeth Leugers, both from Hamilton, Ohio, had migrated to Miami eight years earlier and resided at 3622 S.W. 25th Street. Paul was the proud proprietor of Stegeman Jewelry Store, specializing in watch repair.

Harold Stegeman was a student in the third grade at St. Theresa Elementary School when lung problems compelled him to spend seven days in Miami's Jackson Hospital. The State Department investigation revealed that Harold Stegeman died on November 3, 1945, at the age of eight years, four months, and fourteen days.

State Department investigators suspected that the adult male calling himself Harold Stegeman had also used the alias Frank Wincheski when he purchased photo engraving supplies from Inland Photo Supply Company in Spokane. These supplies were later utilized in a counterfeiting operation run by the man who claimed to be Harold Stegeman.

Be he Frank or Harold, Barb's tall, dashing, and debonair beloved was a creative piece of work: a fraudulently obtained United States passport, fabricated identification and driver's license, hundred dollar bills which he had printed in an Idaho shed, and fingerprints matching those of a respectable, albeit deceased, Portland businessman named Phil Champagne.

Barb Stegeman and her five children had two good reasons to be dismayed. First, she was on trial for passing bogus bills. Second, she had been unceremoniously informed that her husband was counterfeit as well.

"Nothing would surprise me now," wept a sorrowful Mrs. Stegeman to an alternately stunned and bemused jury. "My husband could be involved in murder or anything as far as I know."

Richard Sanger, Barb's court-appointed attorney, outlined her defense in simple terms—she didn't know the bills that Harold had given her were counterfeit. Harold was going to testify in her behalf, but the revelation that Harold wasn't Harold didn't make him an ideal witness.

The jury found Barb Stegeman guilty. Released while she awaited sentencing, Barb and Harold were reunited.

"I married a man, not a name," insisted the loyal spouse of Harold Stegeman. Harold, Frank, Pete, and/or Phil wept with joy.

The Secret Service could tell stories about Harold Stegeman to rival the best pulp adventure fiction, but they won't. That's why they're called the Secret Service.

Created in 1865 as part of the Treasury Department, the Secret Service was established to defend the integrity of United States currency. As any amateur anarchist knows, one of the quickest ways to unravel an economy and the government that backs it is to create one's own unauthorized government issue notes.

Harold Stegeman, however, was not and is not an anarchist, amateur or otherwise, and he will gladly tell stories about the Secret Service, the art of counterfeiting, how to acquire a U.S. passport with fraudulent identification, or helpful survival tips for your next shoot-out with international smugglers. He also knows everything about the strange death of Phil Champagne.

Phil Champagne's children, Kathy, Renee, Phillip Jr., and Curtis, wept during the memorial service held in his honor at Portland's Little Chapel in the Chimes. Phil's younger brother, John Robin, was not invited. He had been the last man to speak to Phil alive and his parting words to Phil were these: "I never want to see you again."

"The day didn't start on such an unpleasant note," notes the once deceased Mr. Champagne. "John Robin, Larry Wills, an old high school pal of Mitch's from Boise, Idaho, and I got together for a few days of boating and fishing in the beautiful San Juan Islands. Mitch also invited our buddy, Ed Grass, but at the last minute, both Mitch and Ed had to cancel out."

"John, Mitch, and Phil Champagne were like real brothers to me," recalls Grass. "They are wonderful, kind, hardworking men who always treated me with the utmost kindness and friendship. I had been with them before on that beautiful forty-two foot Westsail—the *Warlock*—and I was supposed to be with them that weekend. A family matter came up and I couldn't go, but," says Grass with a sigh, "I often wonder if things would have gone differently if Mitch and I had been with the boys that night."

The boys—Phil, Larry, and John—did not travel together to the San Juans.

"Phil called Thursday to say he was meeting Larry Wills and would like to take him fishing and sailing," recounts John Robin. "I explained I had a prior commitment to take Jim Hinson and his family sailing, but that they would return to Portland on Sunday afternoon."

Saturday, Phil drove up Interstate 5 from Portland through Olympia and Tacoma to meet Larry's Saturday flight from Boise at Sea-Tac International. Arriving in Anacortes, Washington, the two men rented a room for the night at the Gateway Motel.

The following day, while they waited for John Robin to arrive, Phil and Larry asked the Gateway's owner, Gerald Simon, for permission to re-enter the room to watch a ball game. They promised not to make a mess or cause any trouble. Mr. Simon agreed.

Uniting at the *Warlock* about an hour after the Hinsons had left, the three men had drinks at The Harbor, a little restaurant on the right side of Main Street going into town.

"Then we picked up a pizza from another place on the same

side of the street," continues John Robin. "They didn't serve any beer or wine, so we went back to the boat to eat the pizza and go to bed."

The next day, after an early breakfast, Larry Wills bought seasick pills in preparation for their afternoon fishing excursion to Cypress Island. Larry didn't get sick, and they caught one sand shark and one small cod.

By nightfall, the hot August day, augmented by chips and beer, had cooled to a balmy island warmth. Phil, Larry, and John Robin returned to Anacortes and tied up in front of Boomer's Landing next to Wyman's Marina overlooking Guemes Channel.

"Phil fell when jumping from the boat to the dock because of his street shoes. I repeatedly tried to get him to wear a pair of my deck shoes," insists John Robin, "but they were a little small for him, so he wouldn't wear them."

Seated in the terraced dining room of Boomer's Landing, the men dined on steaks, chicken, pasta, and salad. Phil and Larry consumed impressive amounts of alcohol while John Robin stayed sober and flirted with cocktail waitress Linda Carlson. He did his best to convince her of the potential benefits of joining them aboard the *Warlock*. Having heard similar pitches and being a married woman, she simply waved good-bye as the three men motored out into the darkness.

Once they returned to the boat, John Robin switched fuel tanks and bled the engine. The winds were light, but he raised the sail to help steady the boat and increase fuel economy. Aboard the *Warlock*, Phil and Larry, over John's objections, began drinking vodka.

"I was a bit drunk, and I know Larry was also. It was a very relaxing day, and I had a marvelous time," relates Champagne, squinting into the horizon as if seeing 1982's San Juan Islands' sunlight dancing and sparkling on the waves. "I enjoyed John, Larry, the weather, the food, the drink. It was the first time I'd had any fun in a long while.

"My wife Joanne and I, after twenty-eight years, had hit significant skids in our relationship. Hell, we had been sliding toward separation for sometime. We would have done it sooner, but a promise is a promise, and I take promises seriously. We waited 'til the kids were grown."

Attorney Don Robertson, a silver-haired Mount Rushmore

of a man who at one time or another has represented almost every member of the Champagne family, describes Joanne Champagne as "a good mother and hardworking woman. She has always been more conservative and down-to-earth than Phil. Perhaps you would call her old-fashioned, more straight-laced. Some might consider her not as refined as Phil or say that they were a mismatched couple or that she is not the type of woman you would imagine to be Phil Champagne's wife. It is true that they had problems, but I have a great deal of respect and affection for Joanne Champagne."

Others are less generous in their appraisal of Phil's ex-better half.

"She was always unpredictable in her responses to situations," observes John Robin, "you never knew what to expect. She could be perfectly sweet and happy one minute and screaming the next. Maybe there was a medical explanation, but it seemed to me that her mood swings were dramatic and intense."

Then again, maybe Phil made her crazy.

"I had seen her verbally abuse him and insult him in public," recalls John Robin, "but because I was so happily married at the time, I couldn't relate to Phil's unhappiness in the relationship. As my brother has never been perfect, I'm sure she had complaints about him, too."

The children were not unaware of their mother's darker side.

"My kids all love their mother very much and would do anything to protect her, but they all know that she can be verbally abusive and say things that cut like a knife. Even they had to be careful not to talk too much because she would get paranoid and accuse them of conspiring against her."

A few years prior to the boating accident, Phil confided to his daughter Renee that he wanted to leave Joanne and begin a new life. The idea was not greeted with enthusiasm.

"She told me that all the kids would hate me forever," says Champagne, "and I am sure they were concerned about what would happen to Joanne if I left."

The Champagne household was never the scene of physical abuse or domestic violence. The backlog of emotional bruises from decades of acerbic tirades resulted only in emotional distance and barren stretches of icy silence.

In June 1980, Phil moved out of the family home at 19202 S.E.

Bel-Air in Clackamas, Oregon, and rented a small apartment in Gresham about ten miles east of the city limits of Portland. After the split, Phil began killing time and assassinating his sensibilities in Portland's night spots.

Downshifting from his usual higher class haunts of the Gresham Golf Course, the Cattle Company, Top of the Cosmos, and the Rusty Pelican to some of the metro area's tougher night spots, he exchanged exaggerated and semifictional adventure stories with the rough and tumble of diverse locales and questionable parentage.

Having seldom walked on the wild side since his restless youth, Phil circled these new acquaintances as would an entomologist approaching a new species of scorpion. Half-lit in the dank glow of piratical rum, acting out against the wine stained backdrop of false front camaraderie, the shiftless, darting-eyed piranhas appeared benignly picaresque.

By the time the music stopped and the bars closed down, Phil had returned to his rented digs. Unlike the swaggering braggarts who provided his evening entertainment, Phil had a real job, reliable income, young adults who called him Dad, and friends in high places. What Phil Champagne shared with these unkempt nocturnals was self-induced internal numbness and the sensation of being buried alive by the future.

Phil's attraction to the sozzled denizens of Portland's soggy underworld was not a desire to be part of them, but to be disconnected from himself. In truth, he saw them for what they were—arrested adolescents delaying the detention of adulthood. At fifty-two, Phil had begun serving the life sentence of assumed maturity long ago.

Working in construction, living in constriction, Phil Champagne appreciated any inference of escape. One night, with deadpanned seriousness, he dutifully wrote down the phone numbers given which offered Phil a possible connection to a man in Mexico.

"The more Jim Beam this guy consumed, the better friend I became," laughs Phil. "I let down my guard and it slipped that I would just as soon start a new life, not that I had any plans to do so, and he said, 'I know a man in Mexico who would probably be happy to have a man like you working for him.'"

The contact was someone who could use a fellow of Phil's

talents and maturity in what sounded to be, at best, a dubious import/export enterprise. Phil did not intend to pursue the recommendation, but it tickled him to know he possessed private phone numbers radiating an aura of successful illegality.

"We didn't know each other that well, but as we had been introduced socially through this character's attorney, a lawyer with whom we both conducted perfectly legal and respectable business, he must have thought I was a real good ol' boy."

The man making the referral fell into the social strata best described as "smudged-collar worker"—white-collar appearance, but with dirt beneath more than his nails. He pretended not to be surprised when Phil asked, "What's the number?"

Champagne took down the area code and particulars on the back of a napkin, stuffed it into his inside pocket for later disposal, and changed the topic.

Three days later, when Phil Champagne pulled the crumpled napkin out of his pocket, he hesitated before throwing it in the trash. "What the hell," Phil thought, and copied the numbers into his address book.

"I can't say why I did it. Maybe it gave me a cheap ego thrill to know I had this guy's number. If he was in the line of business I imagined he was in, he was a definite tare among the listings of wheat."

The episode held sufficient significance for Champagne to share it with his buddy, Alias Mike.

Alias Mike is an alias for damn good reasons. The story of Phil Champagne began with his early and unexpected death, but over the years of his absence, the body count rose.

"Mike said I should have flushed the napkin down the sewer before I left the bar."

Mike was right.

As usual, he understood Phil's mental condition. The two men had shared an unspoken psychic symmetry since their prepubescent bonding as seventh grade classmates in Lake Forest Park, a once rural community north of Seattle.

In April 1946, when fifteen-year-old Phil lied about his age to join the Merchant Marines, Alias Mike was right there with him. So was their school chum, John LeGate, and John LeGate had a younger sister named Joanne. Joanne had no intention of joining the Merchant Marines, but Phil had every intention of joining Joanne.

"My, oh my," says Champagne with a smile, "I thought little Joanne LeGate was a knockout."

Joanne waved good-bye when Phil, Mike, and her brother John shipped out for Europe aboard the *Marine Dragon* in 1946. A year later Phil found himself aboard *Foss Tug LT377* heading for Honolulu to bring back postwar explosives, and on November 8, 1949, Phil Champagne married Joanne LeGate in a simple ceremony at a preacher's home in Ridgecrest, Washington.

"Joanne was a beautiful bride and," he adds with a hint of impishness, "she was only a little bit pregnant."

Having returned to their old stomping grounds, Phil and his new brother-in-law's stomping quickly got out of hand. On November 27, 1950, the hell-raising, twenty-year-old boys went on a late night spree, upending tombstones and breaking windows. The King County authorities were not amused. LeGate and Champagne were apprehended, fingerprinted, and charged with property damage. They were ordered to make restitution and donate one hundred dollars to Orthopedic Hospital.

It was agreed that it would be best if the boys shipped out. Phil finished out 1950 working in Washington's Christmas tree harvest, and in 1951 he and John LeGate sailed aboard the *General Greeley* through the Panama Canal to New York City. As advised, they took a long, leisurely train ride from the East Coast back to the state of Washington.

And like The Cat in the Hat, the boys came back. Phil Champagne returned as restless, rowdy, and charming as when he was fifteen, with an emphasis on restless and rowdy, the natural consequences of Phil Champagne's haphazard upbringing.

Born in Seattle, the product of the stormy union of Eli and Anita Champagne, Phil's parents were separated at the time of his birth. Fourteen years later, Eli and Anita were officially divorced. Phil and his brothers were raised in poverty and relied on welfare grants for support and constantly shifted from one home to another.

Anita Champagne and her middle son did not exemplify the finer points of family unity, and fifteen-year-old Phil was referred to the Seattle Guidance Clinic in 1945 because of problems with his mother. With her blessing, he joined the Merchant Marines in an attempt to jump start adulthood. By the early 1950s, Phil was supposed to be a grownup.

"I was a married man with a family to support, but I behaved like an irresponsible teenager," admits Champagne. "I hadn't matured a whit. And to prove it, on June 9, 1953, I got drunk and took someone's new car for an extended joyride. When I was done with it, I parked it and walked away. The next morning, when I sobered up, I couldn't find my wallet. I went back to the car to see if I had left it there. It turned out I had left my wallet at the gas station when I bought a buck's worth of gas. The gas station attendant turned it over to the cops, who then staked out the car. So, there I was, under arrest."

And guilty as hell.

This time, however, he wasn't a wild teen knocking over tombstones, he was an adult who had been caught taking a motor vehicle without authorization. His wife was furious, the judge was not sympathetic, and Phil was sentenced to one year at the correctional institute in Monroe, Washington.

As far as Joanne was concerned, the timing, not to mention the behavior, could not have been worse. Their first child, Kathy, was only a toddler, and Joanne was pregnant with their second.

"Being sent to Monroe was a life-changing experience," admits Champagne. "I grew up in a hurry. Renee was born while I was behind bars and that really had an impact on me. It was like slapping me upside the head. You never saw a guy change so fast in your life."

Released from Monroe a model of contrition, a far more mature Phil Champagne migrated to Oregon with his family and joined Mitch as an employee of Carnation Dairy.

"Phil was one amazing milkman," laughs John Robin, implying that Phil's delivery route was an unending symphony of rattling bottles and squeaking bedsprings.

Becoming a licensed pasteurizer, Phil devoted ten good years to Arden Farms before following John Robin into construction.

Phil built homes while he and Joanne expanded their family. After four children and nearly three decades of marriage, the family painfully collapsed as the housing market did the same.

In 1982 Phil Champagne was no longer a teenager. He was over fifty, his unrelenting optimism and self-confidence were beginning to ebb, and his friends were concerned.

"It was easy to see that Phil was becoming increasingly stressed out, and needed a few fun-filled days of fishing, sunshine, and friendship," remembers Ed Grass, "and we all hoped that the late August trip to the San Juans would do the trick."

The trick was not what anyone expected.

"When we started slicing through the night water I felt like a free man," says Champagne wistfully. "There we were, a little tipsy, out on the water. I don't remember our destination, but we were near the Straits of Juan de Fuca. I had sneaked another bottle of vodka on board and was still drinking. John Robin didn't like folks getting drunk on the boat, but I didn't get much of a chance to cut loose and have a good time. So what if Larry and I got a little drunk?"

Even the most pleasant evening, fermented in enough alcohol, will turn sour. Old-timers have a name for it: The Darker Drink—the one shot that puts the pall of death on a lively night, turns fellowship into fistfights, loosens petty demons stuck in men's craws, and sets brother against brother.

"Somehow we got on the subject of Mitch's latest construction project—the Cottonwood Condominium development in a Portland suburb. There had been severe cost overruns because of some drainage problems which we had not anticipated. I was the one to oversee the site, so according to John, it was my oversight." Phil pauses for a moment of reflection. "It was a stupid discussion for two brothers, one of them rather tipsy, to be having in front of a friend on a boat in the dark at night. Had Mitch been there he would have told us both to shut up."

Phil peered blearily at John Robin through the dark, weaving in rhythm with the rocking boat.

"You're trying to make Mitch's problems all my fault," declared Phil with the conviction of a man inebriated. "Don't blame me for things I can't control."

Blame is important to drunks and lawyers.

"The last thing I remember John saying," recalls Phil, "is that he didn't want to see me again. He turned and started to go either below or to the wheel. He stopped and turned back to look at me."

"D'ya know what?" John, despite his sobriety, let the Darker Drink speak. "If the truth were known, I don't think any of the others in the family want to see you again either."

John certainly knew how to put a positive cap on a night of carefree camaraderie.

"I did tend to criticize Phil," acknowledges John Robin, "but I don't recall my recriminations being that severe. I usually knew just how far I could push Phil before he got mad or hurt, because Phil was very easygoing and slow to anger. Quite often my faultfinding would do him some good. We did have that conversation, and I did say those things, but I think that the alcohol amplified the intensity with which he experienced it. If he'd taken my repeated insistence that he put on deck shoes as seriously as he took my remarks about his role in the construction site problems, he might not have gone over the side."

Phil, sozzled, silent, and still in his street shoes, turned toward the stern. He really didn't know where he was going.

He went overboard.

When John Robin caught the brief blur of Phil falling, he wasn't immediately concerned.

"My initial reaction was 'well, that's going to wake his ass up, hitting that cold water.' I stopped the boat, turned it around, and thought I would be able to see him right away."

He didn't.

John Robin grabbed a handheld searchlight and jumped down from the wheel, still confident that he would see Phil at any moment.

"I couldn't see him anywhere. I had a life ring on the back of the boat and a strobe light. I took the damn life ring, attached the strobe light, turned it on, and dropped it in to mark the spot. I was worried about the current and how we were drifting. Then I went below and called the Coast Guard, told them that I had a man overboard, had marked the spot, and that we were circling. It took them between twenty minutes and an hour to show up."

Larry Wills, previously pleasantly inebriated, was transformed into a panic-stricken drunk on deck.

"He was out of it, frantic, and flailing around. I was afraid Larry was going to fall overboard also. But he got a grip on himself in a hurry, and even though he had been drinking heavily, was able to steer. He suggested we shut the engine off and sail whenever possible so we would hear better if Phil was yelling."

The Coast Guard helicopter was aided in its search by the cutter *Polar Sea*. The search lasted thirteen hours.

Recalling the details of that agonizing night, John Champagne fights back a flood of conflicting emotions.

"I know now that it wasn't real, that he didn't die. But it was real to me then; real to me every day and every night since it happened. I have relived all of it over and over again, year after year. The fear, the prayers, the grief. I've gone over every detail of that night in my mind a thousand times," laments John Champagne. "What could I have done differently, how could I have saved my brother's life?"

There were several fishing boats in the immediate vicinity, but only one of them displayed interest in the search by assisting the *Polar Sea.*

"After the first hour," John's voice stalls as the memory constricts his larynx, "I knew that we were only looking for a body."

Even sober, an athletic swimmer can be deceived to death in dark waters, explained the Coast Guard. Rather than relaxing and floating to the surface, the natural inclination is to swim against the resistance toward safety. Phil Champagne, it was speculated, swam down rather than up. In truth, Phil Champagne didn't swim anywhere at all.

"I remember hitting the water, but if I had a near-death experience I was too drunk to remember it. I do recall wondering if this is what it was like for Dad."

Champagne's father, Eli Mitchell Champagne, drowned in Washington's Blue Lake when Phil was in his teens.

"If my life was going to pass before my eyes, I wasn't that interested," quips Phil. "I have never been a fan of reruns, and it wasn't that great the first time around."

Sometimes men make light of what is most important. Phil didn't see the light, he only saw meaningless humdrum repetition in his ordered, rapidly vanishing life as he sank into wet, relentless darkness.

"What had I ever done that was worth a damn? What had I accomplished in my life? Nothing, I thought, nothing at all. Get married, have kids, raise kids, get old, get sick, die. Big deal."

No one is about to offer Phil Champagne a counseling job at a hospice, but it was his life, his death, his self-evaluation.

"If I had died, it was no big loss. I felt that what came next must at least be different."

Phillip Champagne stared death in the face and found the face of a ten-year-old boy staring back.

"Hey, Mom. The man woke up," the boy said.

Champagne's consciousness resurfaced in a child's bedroom. Phil saw toys and other obvious indications of preadolescence, an odd collection of stuffed animals and posters of popular sports figures. Phil had seen these same things in his own boys' rooms.

When his youngest son, Curtis, turned twenty, he had stopped looking at Daddy with the same eyes. Since the breakup, he had hardly looked at him at all. If there was blame to be attached, Phil was no longer drunk enough to attach it.

The child's attractive, fortysomething mother appeared briefly in the doorway. She smiled, turned, and walked away. Phil heard her use the phone. He knew it was a phone. He recognized the rotary dial.

"Rotary dial. Rotary dial. The name sounds exactly like what it is," Phil spoke to himself, but his lips didn't move. "If you say 'rotary dial' there is exactly one click for every letter; it takes the exact amount of time to say 'rotary dial' as it does to dial the zero."

He attempted to sit up.

He failed.

He tried to call out but was not sure if sound escaped his throat. For a moment he wondered if he was invisible, but then recalled both the child and the woman had seen him. It had seemed a reasonable question when it first occurred to him. Maybe he had the flu. Maybe he was delirious. Maybe he was dead. It was too complicated.

The boy continued to stare at the rumpled man, while the man stared at the ceiling. The kid-sized bed barely contained the long, lanky frame of Phil Champagne. The little boy had never seen a man sleep with his eyes open before. The man must be asleep, the child reasoned, because dead men don't cough, moan, and call out names.

"I see you're back among the living." A cheerful male voice commanded Phil's attention and dominated the room. Champagne blinked, bringing his open eyes into focus. He didn't know the voice, didn't know the face. He didn't have the slightest idea where on earth he was.

"At first we thought you were dead."

Champagne's mind attempted to unravel the intricacies of the situation, but the situation wasn't all that intricate. A bearded, roughhewn man in jeans, Pendleton shirt, and black boots filled the doorway with his broad shoulders. Flipping open a Zippo, the man brought the bluish flame to the Lucky Strike trapped between his lips. Phil, after the first decade or the first puff, whichever came sooner, understood that the smoking bearded man was attempting to make conversation.

"You must be Art," mumbled Phil stupidly.

"Art?" The man in the door with smoke pouring out his nose didn't understand.

"Art of Lost Conversation." Phil hated explaining a joke.

"You've been here almost four days," offered the beard. "When I first found you, I thought you was dead. You know I fished you out of the water, right?"

Oh, yeah, the water. It was starting to come off pause and slip into rewind. Playback and pay backs were imminent.

Reclining beneath a poster of Luke Skywalker, Phil propped himself up on his elbows as if a clear line of sight would encourage his brain to realign as well.

"Why didn't you…?" Phil wasn't sure what he was about to ask.

"Take you to a hospital? Well, there's a reason for that. In fact, a couple of good reasons," the bearded, smoking dragon of the doorway spit a piece of errant tobacco from the tip of his tongue. "I had fish and plenty of 'em, but I am not exactly authorized to be catchin' 'em, if you understand. I was willing to save your life, but not willing to maybe lose my boat."

"I could have died," Phil intended a manly bark but gave out only a weak, watery yelp. "Exactly where am I?"

"Anacortes, Washington, or at least reasonably close to it. We're not that far from town. Here, you might want to take a look at this." Pulling a newspaper from under his arm, the bearded fisherman stepped forward. Champagne looked to where the man pointed. "Seems like folks figure you're dead."

It was hard for Phil to focus his attention, let alone his vision, but he understood without having to read the details.

"You didn't have no wallet, but you're the only missing man I know of that ain't missing in this house, so that is you, right?"

"I need to use the phone. I gotta tell somebody I'm alive," Phil's voice bore equal traces of desperation and disorientation.

"No phone here," the beard lied. "Tomorrow you can call from town. Your clothes are dry and so's your money."

Phil had forgotten about the money. He always kept cash in his pocket, figuring it was easier to lose your wallet than your pants.

"We don't steal in this family. Helping ourselves to fish provided by nature is one thing, lifting a helpless man's cash is another. And we ain't askin' you to give us any of it neither. Just keep it between us that you was ever here."

"Yeah..." Phil wondered if it was a delirium-induced delusion or if he was really having a conversation.

"You look like your driftin', pal. You sleep some more, and in the morning I'll take you into Anacortes and you can give your people a call or whatever suits you."

Phil leaned back and closed his eyes. "I'll need a shave..."

Whatever additional considerations he was about to voice disappeared in the darkness of exhaustion.

Two

Life being what it is in our world, the onset of death is often the first taste a man gets of freedom.

—Isaac Rosenfeld

Eighty hours after the United States Coast Guard called off its thirteen-hour search for John Champagne's missing brother, the assumed deceased was awakened by the aromas of sizzling bacon, fried eggs, and fresh brewed coffee.

Phil Champagne—showered, shaved, and dressed—cleaned his plate and heard the insistent jingle of the bearded man's keys well before he had swallowed his final triangle of toast. If this was the bum's rush, at least the bum was well fed.

The fisherman's old blue pickup rattled along the blacktop road into the Fidalgo Island city of Anacortes. The beard noted that it was easy to forget that Anacortes was on an island as the bridges connecting it to the mainland made the transition appear seamless. Except for the brief exchange about the geography of the area, the balance of the ride consisted of interpersonal silence punctuated by an occasional gear grind or the metallic flip of the Zippo.

"This is it," said the beard with stoic finality as he pulled over to a downtown curb. "You never saw me; I never saw you."

"Yeah."

Phil yanked at the passenger side's reluctant handle, opened the dented door, and stepped out. He stood for a moment, shifting his weight awkwardly, not quite knowing what to say to the man who had saved his life. As words didn't come, he didn't say anything. The blue pickup simply moved on down the road.

"Okay, so I didn't thank the guy. Looking back, I can see that I wasn't thinking with perfect clarity. I was irked at him for not taking me to the hospital. I could have died there in his cabin, but as he said, 'You're alive, ain't ya, so what are ya complainin' about?'"

Phil watched the pickup become a distant blue blur and turned his attention back to himself. He needed a change of clothes, transportation, and a clear head. Despite more than three days of bed rest, his weariness amazed him. Limp pasta legs and an unrelenting lightheadedness compelled Phil to wobble when he walked. He stopped every half block to steady himself.

"It's not like I had any idea where I was going. There I was, weaving around like a man either going into or coming out of shock, no ID, and a pocketful of cash. On top of all that, I'm missing and presumed dead."

In the mind of his daughter, Renee, Phil was missing and presumed murdered. Following the news of her father's death, she placed an emotional call to the United States Coast Guard alleging that her Uncle John plotted to kill Phil for the insurance money. As John was not a beneficiary of any policy, but Renee was, her accusation was summarily discounted. Later, coming to her senses, Renee apologized to her Uncle John.

Her mother, however, retained Don Robertson to sue John Robin for negligence in the wrongful death of Phil Champagne. Joanne was awarded $8,500 in an out-of-court settlement.

"On top of the pain of losing my brother," recounts John Robin, "I had to deal with accusations of murder and lawsuits of negligence. One day I'm taking my brother and a friend for a boat ride, the next I'm treated like a criminal."

It is no crime to be alive. The Anacortes police had received no APB to be on the lookout for a law-abiding, waterlogged refugee from the briny deep, answering the description of Phillip Wendell Champagne, weaving down Commercial Avenue with $1400 in his pocket.

Phil aimed his unsteady gait toward the first visible coffee shop, sat down in an available booth, and attempted deep thoughts. His success was spotty at best.

"I think that's when it hit me," says Phil. "I remembered that last painful conversation with John; 'it's all your fault, everything is your fault, all of Mitch's problems are your fault, we never want to see you again,' and all that crap. Well, it pissed me off and I was like a kid who decides to take his ball and go home or grabs his teddy bear and a peanut butter sandwich and starts walking, except I wasn't a kid. Yeah, that was it, all right—if they didn't want to see me again, they sure as hell didn't have to."

Before a man can steal, he has to lie; before a man can lie, he has to justify it to himself. Phil Champagne spent the better part of his time in Anacortes engrossed in justifications.

"I figured no one would starve to death if I wasn't around. I was leaving my wife and kids, but she didn't like me anyway. As far as I was concerned, she made my life a living hell. She probably felt the same about me. She accused me of every sin in the book. I have to admit that I wasn't the best husband in the world, but I did provide. Damn right. I always provided. As for the kids, they were grown-up and I managed to convince myself that they wouldn't care if I came home or not."

Champagne's voice catches briefly.

"I love them all," admits Phil. "I knew I would miss them, but I pushed the discomforting thought that I would regret what I was doing to the back of my mind. I didn't want to go back to things the way they were. It was like I had been pulled out of the game and set on the sidelines. It was either go back on the field or leave the stadium."

Phil paid for the coffee, aimed for the exit, and ambled off in search of a clothing store.

"I bought three pairs of Haggar slacks, shirts, socks, underwear, belt, and a good pair of shoes. Then I picked out a small travel bag, packed it neatly, and added basic toiletries. By the time I started thumbing my way from Anacortes to Interstate 5, I was the cleanest, freshest, most affable looking hitchhiker you ever saw in your life."

Champagne got a quick lift to the I-5 southbound on-ramp. With his nonthreatening adult demeanor, crisp clothes, and fresh look, a nonstop ride down the freeway to Seattle was no challenge.

A gregarious salesman in a four-door Oldsmobile attempted entertaining his appreciative passenger with wholesale anecdotes and off-color jokes while Phil deflected any direct questions as to his point of origin or final destination with vague generalities or hastily invented specifics. As a good host senses the discomfort of silence, the driver attempted to fill the void with a contemporary FM soundtrack.

Static.

"That's because of the shading effect of hills and trees," explained the driver. "The FM radio signals hit 'em and drop like a rock. Now, the old AM stations' signals will bounce around forever. They never go away. Send 'em out today, and even if it is a little, tiny 250-watt station, it never goes away; it just keeps bouncing. Why, I bet if you sat down late at night with a real strong AM radio, you could hear old shows from the 1930s still floating back to earth."

"I must be one of those old AM signals," joked Phil Champagne, and the salesman laughed.

The conversation waned, the radio reception improved, and the two men rolled down the interstate past Marysville, Everett, and Mukilteo in air-conditioned comfort. On the outskirts of Lynwood, 96.5 FM cranked out "Heard it on the X."

Even Phil Champagne knew about the infamous "X," a radio station in Mexico with more power in its tower than any station in the U.S.A. Wolfman Jack used to be on the "X" selling autographed pictures of Jesus Christ.

Mexico sounded like Phil's kind of place.

The Oldsmobile hit heavier traffic passing Seattle's Northgate exit, slowed considerably by N.E. 85th, picked up briefly approaching the university district, slowed again at the 520 Interchange, and eased up as they took the Stewart-Denny exit to downtown.

"You can just let me off anywhere here," said Phil. His stomach felt tight. Seattle was civilization in the way that Portland was civilization. Being unconscious, or in Anacortes, was like a respite in the *Twilight Zone*. Phil Champagne wasn't sure he was ready for reentry into reality.

"Hey, the bus depot is just down there. No problem, pal."

Handshakes, thanks, and a solid door slam later, Phil Champagne was standing in front of the Greyhound bus depot.

He walked in, looked around for the schedule, and discovered he had a good two hours until the next bus to Portland, Oregon.

"There was a little restaurant in the bus depot, or attached to it on the west side of the building on the corner, and I sat there drinking coffee and wondering if I was doing the right thing, whatever the hell that was."

Phil purchased a one-way ticket to Portland, pumped a handful of change into a nearby pay phone, and dialed a number in Oregon, area code 503. He didn't call his estranged wife; he didn't call his kids, mother, or brothers. He called Alias Mike.

"If his wife had answered, I would have hung up and tried later," confirms Champagne, "but Mike picked up the phone. To say he was surprised to hear from me would be putting it mildly."

Mike was surprised to hear from his dead best friend, but not surprised by Phil's decision to stay dead.

"At first, Mike wasn't sure it was really me. I told him everything that happened, or at least everything I could remember, and then I told him what I was going to do—stay dead and start over. I will never forget his response, 'It's about time you got out of that hellhole you're in anyway.'"

If Phil Champagne was seeking external validation of his decision to change his life, he got it on the pay phone. Whatever doubts lingered were dispelled the moment Mike uttered the word hellhole. That cinched it.

"We made plans to meet and set the location. I felt giddy when I climbed on the bus to Portland. The ride seemed to take forever, stopping at every would-be depot down the I-5 corridor."

Tacoma, Fort Lewis, Olympia, Centralia, Longview, Vancouver; the opportunities to change his mind outnumbered the rest stops.

"I didn't believe I could change my mind. Once I was on that bus my only goal was to get two things from Portland—my address book and more money."

If there was anything unusual about the well-dressed passenger's behavior when he stepped off the Portland bus, it was only the intensity with which he walked directly to the stately Benson Hotel.

"Mike was waiting for me in a dark corner at the back of Trader Vic's. He shook my hand, stared at me for a bit, and asked what I wanted first, advice or money. I told him I would take as much of both as he was willing to give."

It wasn't true. Phil wanted money and affirmation. He had seen a vision of his life with icelike clarity. In a posttraumatic epiphany reserved for the mystic and the head-injured, he had broken the bonds and snapped the trap. Phil Champagne flew the coop of conventional expectations, embraced the implications of his own demise, and canceled his subscription to the resurrection.

Mike took a good look at his old pal Phil. The man had changed. There was an aura of renewed confidence. This was not the Phil Champagne he had recently seen sinking into a black hole of self-recrimination somewhere in Gresham. Champagne appeared a man possessed.

"It could have been worse," reasoned Mike, "at least he wasn't screaming about Jesus."

Mike correctly observed that Phil Champagne was not truly back from the dead; he was only dropping by for drinks.

"Sure, you can go away, change your name, start a new life somewhere. Maybe. But what about money, a job, a career? You are rapidly approaching old age." Mike laughed as if he were teasing. He wasn't. "You are over fifty."

Phil had his answer prepared, if not rehearsed, and didn't mind waiting for the Trader Vic's waiter to take their order before unloading his litany.

"Remember Smudge Collar, the import/export guy who said he knew where I could get a job?" Phil smiled as if he need say no more.

"Bullshit, Phil," insisted Mike. "That was pure, unadulterated bullshit—bullshit offer and bullshit for you to take down that number. You've got to be kidding."

"What do you mean, bullshit? He wouldn't have given me the number if he didn't mean for me to use it." Phil was convincing himself even as he spoke, pausing to allow the waiter to deliver his vodka and Mike's bourbon. "I want you to go to the condo I was building for Mitch and get my little book. It has a number I can call in Mexico City. I'll tell you exactly where my book is."

Mike banged his glass on the table, spilling a puddle beside the cocktail napkin. He looked around and wiped his mouth with thumb and forefinger, stalling to stay calm.

"Honest to God, Phil. You better sleep on this. Besides," hissed Mike, "I'm not going out to those damn condos in the middle of the fucking night. I'll get it early in the morning, but I want you to get some sleep. Then we'll get you out of town."

"Yeah, get me out of town for sure. I don't want to hang around here. Shit, if someone sees me, I'll be a dead man."

They laughed at Phil's unintentioned humor, breaking the tension born of emotional disagreement.

"I'll drive you to Salem in the morning, and you can catch the bus to wherever it is you wanna go from there."

"I just want to go…" For a fraction of a moment Phillip Champagne didn't have the slightest idea.

He attempted to form the sentence again.

"I just want to go someplace where I can feel okay, never have to deal with Joanne again, and never do anything to piss off or disappoint my family, Mitch, John—anybody."

"I guess if gone, you can't do anything wrong," Mike commented dryly.

"Right about that," Phil agreed seriously "I am never, ever, again going to be in a position where someone can say Mitch's problems are all my fault. As for marriage…"

"Easy, Phil. I'm a happily married man. My wife and I get along fine."

Champagne snapped a swizzle stick between his fingers.

"That's right, Mike, rub it in. You are one in a million. I bet there are hundreds of thousands of men and women out there right now who feel just as I did before I died. Trapped, suffocated, tormented, blamed, shamed…," Phil ran out of words.

"Try reamed and creamed and a bit obscene," suggested Mike helpfully. Phil laughed and raised his glass in a silent toast.

"You're a good friend, Mike. I've got other good friends, too—Don Robertson, Ed Grass—but please don't tell them I'm alive. And for God's sake, don't tell my brothers."

"I'm not telling a single living soul as long as I live," vowed Mike. "Want another drink?"

"No," said Phil, soaking up Mike's spillage with the little Trader Vic's napkin, "I wouldn't want to go overboard."

"Yeah, overboard," chuckled Mike. "Speaking of which, don't go running away from one bad patch of aggravation into another with this Mexico deal. Watch your step. I don't want you to end up dead or making license plates. After all, your style has always been more Sheraton than Shelton."

Phil understood the alliterative reference easily enough. Shelton, population seventy-two hundred, located on an inlet of South Puget Sound near Olympia, Washington, is famed for Christmas trees, succulent oysters, and a penal institution called the Washington Correction Center.

Phil had never attended the Shelton Octoberfest oyster-shucking contest and considered "Correction Center" an absurd euphemism. What would they correct? Your spelling? Your golf swing? Phil was, however, intimately familiar with Shelton's Christmas tree harvest. Between late November and mid-December 1950, Phil cut, packaged, and shipped a portion of the three million Christmas trees exported from Shelton to happy homes throughout the region.

"I know the difference between Sheraton and Shelton," said Phil, "but do you know the difference between a sailor and a shower?"

"No."

"Well, you better find out before you get under one."

Mike laughed more from obligation than spontaneity. The conversation concluded and the drinks paid for, Phil and Mike arranged to meet in the morning then split up.

With neither a Sheraton or Shelton in sight, Phil Champagne, using an assumed name, checked into the Hilton down the street, went up to the rather elegant room, and slid between the cool cotton sheets. In the morning, Mike would drive him to Salem, see him off with warm wishes and cold cash, and he would be free—free from providing, free from blame, free from responsibility for anyone or anything except himself.

On that September night in 1982, Phil Champagne slept the sleep of a man at peace. The Hilton was even better than the Sheraton, and both were better than Shelton.

Barbara LeHew Yokum Fraley of Olympia, Washington, was not so fortunate. Her sleep that night was fitful at best. As always, she said her prayers with heartfelt sincerity. That's the way she was raised—believe in the Bible and trust in God. Her upbringing was strict, religious, unflinching, and crowded—four brothers, two sisters, one mother, and no father.

Barb had become accustomed to hardship, but it was not her personal preference. She was never afraid of hard work, but she was becoming pretty darn tired of it.

She prayed for her kids; she prayed for herself. But, in the final analysis, it was up to her to provide for the five children from her failed thirteen-year marriage to former Shelton inmate #222301, Richard Yokum, a.k.a. Richard Fraley.

When Barb married Richard Yokum in 1965, no one thought the naive, estrogen-crazed eighteen-year-old girl had made the catch of the century. He was a soldier from Fort Lewis with a passion for the ladies and a proclivity for going AWOL. They met in 1964 at the Evergreen Ballroom, where Barb worked part-time in the cafeteria. The night Buck Owens performed, Barb had the evening off and Richard discovered the girl of his dreams on the dance floor.

"Oh, he was a good-looking fellow, all right," says Barb with a laugh. "My mother forbid me to marry until I was eighteen. I was seventeen when I met Richard and fell madly in love. We were married a year later."

Richard was on probation.

"He had taken a succession of unsuccessful jobs after the Army invited him to leave," recounts Barb, "one of them being for a janitorial service which cleaned department stores, except Richard didn't just clean them, he cleaned them out—he stole a television and some other items and pawned them. Not a smart move, and he got in big trouble."

That wasn't the end of it.

One year after Richard promised to love, honor, and cherish her forever, Barb was eight months pregnant with their first child and facing a prison sentence for forgery. Both the pregnancy and forgery were, according to Barb, the doings of Richard Yokum.

"He stole a woman's purse from a bowling alley, took the cash, and wanted me to sign her name for purchases using her credit card," relates Barb, minimizing her blatant criminal complicity. "When I was supposed to sign, I chickened out and ran out of the store. It was too late. They got me for forgery or attempted forgery or something. Then they came after me for stealing the purse. It wasn't me that stole the purse," insists Barb, "it was Richard."

Richard recalled the purse stealing incident as a collaborative effort.

"Had she not been with me," he admits, "she would not have done it on her own."

"I was a foolish girl and up to no good," recalls the ex-Mrs. Yokum. "I can't say what sterling qualities I first saw in Richard besides his good looks and charming personality, but what I got from Richard right off the bat were pregnancy and imprisonment."

Barb insisted her lawyer begged her to name Richard the father as Richard the purse snatcher.

"But he'll go to jail," objected Barb.

"That," her lawyer explained, "is the whole idea."

Richard Yokum, who was already on probation, provided convincing descriptions of dire consequences for both her and the child should he be sent away.

Barb's lawyer talked her out of pleading guilty, launching a defense of innocent by reason of insanity. "He figured I had to be nuts," explained Barb ruefully.

The day her first baby was born, Barb went off for ten months to the county jail to await trial. The baby went off with Barb's mother. Barb got probation.

Richard Yokum's attempts to avoid incarceration proved equally fruitless. While Barb was in the county jail, he violated probation. Richard Yokum was sent to the correction center in Shelton. After release he violated parole and spent a year at the correction center in Monroe, Washington, where Phil had stayed in the early fifties, followed by a stay at the Washugal Honor Camp in 1971.

"Richard had been using the name Yokum because that was his grandparents' name, and they raised him," explains Barb. "But it turned out his legal name was Fraley, and that was the name on the baby's birth certificate, too. All of a sudden I was Mrs. Fraley instead of Mrs. Yokum. When he applied for a job with the Washington State Department of Institutions in 1971, he did so as Richard Fraley."

The new and improved Richard worked the first three years as a counselor at the Rainier State School in Buckley, Washington, for what were then termed "retarded kids." He was then transferred to a similar position at Cascadia Diagnostic Center, a residential program for troubled juveniles. When Cascadia closed down, Richard Fraley relocated to Shelton's Washington

Correction Center, but this time not as an inmate.

If a leopard can't change its spots, Richard Yokum Fraley is the exceptional leopard. He became an exemplary employee of the Washington Correction Center, if not a model husband, and built a rewarding career highlighted by consistent pay raises and promotions.

With Richard Fraley on the right side of the law, a good job, and promising future, things should have been peachy between Richard and Barb. He was, after all, an excellent provider. He was also a handsome devil who had a way with the ladies. The problem was in the plurality. According to Barb, Richard became increasingly indiscreet about where he parked his nightstick. After thirteen years of marriage, Barb and Richard agreed to divorce.

"As a mature, sober adult, Richard is not a bad guy at all," comments Barb. "I have no malice toward him. He never beat me, abused me, or anything like that, and when we were married, he always provided well for the kids and me. Maybe he was just too good-looking for his own good. When Richard and I split up, it wasn't easy for anybody."

And Barb kept working. Her mother was in the restaurant business, and Barb knew her way around a kitchen. She worked two or three different jobs at once to support the kids.

Overworked, underpaid, and longing for true love, Barb Fraley, against her mother's deathbed wishes, remarried on April 30, 1983. The man was Cecil Chapman. Together, he and Barb moved to Shelton, where her new husband joined Richard on the right side of the bars at the Correction Center, becoming her ex-husband's drinking buddy.

"I was the one in the wedding dress," quips Barb, "but Cecil wound up with Richard."

After three years of what Barb terms "irreconcilable differences" fueled by Cecil's excessive alcohol consumption, there was nothing she wanted from Chapman except away. She didn't even retain his name. The kids were all Fraleys, so she stayed one, too.

A five-time mother and two-time divorcee, Barb never had the opportunity to take it easy. Since leaving Olympia's Washington Junior High at the age of fifteen to attend the live-in nurse's aide program at Saint Peter's Hospital, her life had been nonstop work punctuated by pregnancy, imprisonment, infidelity, and abuse. As a professional victim, Barb was ready for a career change.

In March 1986, while tending bar at Shelton's roadside Cottage Cafe, she met Harold Richard Stegeman. A tall, handsome man, his refined bearing marked him immediately as someone whose origin and upbringing were far removed from that of the locals. Harold was a man with class.

On his first visit to the Cottage Cafe, Harold sat with a local real estate agent hacking out the details for the sale of a cabin he was building on nearby Harstein Island. On subsequent visits, Harold found more delight in the presence of Ms. Fraley than in any item on the menu. They had short, relaxed chats as she refilled his coffee. He spoke of the cabin he was building and his recent retirement from a successful career in Florida real estate. He had never been married, never had kids. Wistfully, Barb dreamed that she could change that part of his story.

Three weeks after their initial encounter, Harold waited around the Cottage Cafe until Barb's shift was over to ask her out on a Friday night date. She hesitated a few seconds before responding—not from doubt as to her answer, but out of complete surprise.

"When Harold asked me out, I was in total shock. I never in a million years thought he would look at me twice. My self-esteem was gone. I no longer considered myself attractive, and I was nobody but the mother of five children."

Flattered, she joyously accepted.

Pensive about his acceptance of her five children, she made no mention of them during their first few evenings together. In time Barb decided to reveal their existence, but prefaced her self-conscious disclosure with the observation that Harold might not ever want to date her again once he knew "the truth."

"I have five kids," Barb told him holding up her hand with all five fingers spread wide, "and I do mean five."

Barb held her breath. Harold laughed. He already knew. When he had picked her up for their first date, he saw the noses pressed against the front window. Harold could count.

After six months of romantic dating, Harold, Barb, and the remaining three minor children began cohabitation. Harold treated her with respect, cared for her deeply, and was seriously concerned for her needs and the well-being of her children. For the first time since her mid-teens, Barb didn't have to work. Her kids, accustomed to scraping by, hardly knew how to act around the kind, loving man who found simple, honest pleasure in making them happy.

Harold Stegeman built a house in the Mud Bay area near Olympia, sold it at a profit, and then, knowing Barb had an extensive background in restaurant and lounge management, financed Barb's Country Kitchen and Stegey's Blue Room just off the main highway between Shelton and Bremerton on Spencer Lake. Barb felt the remote location posed a significant risk, but Harold was convinced that the site was perfect for tourist traffic. Stegeman firmly believed that a well-run restaurant featuring delicious prime rib would be like having a license to print money.

With construction beginning on the restaurant, Harold bought a twenty-eight foot Mercruiser inboard/outboard Tollycraft boat so they would have something to do while their new venture was being built. They took the kids fishing all day and spent the night on the boat. The next morning they would find a nice place on the water to eat and enjoy a leisurely breakfast. Barb LeHew Fraley's prayers were no longer pleas for help, but prayers of praise and gratitude for the blessing in her life named Harold Stegeman.

The restaurant opened with hoopla and fanfare in October 1987. The food was delicious, the drinks generous, the service adequate, and Harold Stegeman became Shelton's resident high-profile tycoon. Everyone knew his story: "Mr. Moneybags fell in love with the local waitress and built her a restaurant all her own."

Soon after the grand opening, Harold also bought Barb a lovely five-bedroom house on the lake and a new car. On the weekends, Harold and Barb would travel to Seattle where he introduced her to the Sheraton Towers, Trader Vic's, and the famous Thirteen Coins.

"I had never been to places like that in my life," recalls Barb, "I felt like Cinderella at the ball. On New Year's Eve, Harold took me to a party at the Seattle Sheraton. He wore a tuxedo and had me fitted for an evening gown. An evening gown!" Barb repeats with a delightful combination of astonishment and glee.

Mom was right. Life was good. Believe in the Bible, trust in God, and good things come to those who wait. If it was a dream, Barb LeHew Fraley Stegeman never wanted to wake up. She would never go back. She was free at last—free to relax, free to enjoy, free to be the loving partner of Harold Richard Stegeman.

❦ ❦ ❦

With the sun streaming through the windows of the downtown Portland Hilton, the world was bright with infinite possibilities for the newly awakened Phil Champagne. Room service delivered a delicious breakfast with plenty of fresh brewed coffee, and Phil had let the hot shower beat on his back for an eternity before getting out and drying off. He picked out a pair of the new Haggar slacks and a shirt from the wardrobe he had hung carefully in the closet of the Hilton, buffed his new shoes, and whistled while he packed his travel bag. Walking to the window, Phil Champagne took in the view.

Portland looked more like Portland than ever—half a million people living in what was first called Stumptown. The name "Portland" was decided by an 1845 coin toss. If the coin had landed the other side up, Phil Champagne would be hightailing it out of Boston, Oregon, instead of Portland.

Just for the hell of it, Phil flipped a coin. Heads it's Portland, tails it's Boston. Boston won.

"Shows what I know," said Phil. He pocketed the coin, picked up his bag, paid up, checked out, and met Mike right on time in the passenger load zone.

"Did you get my little book?"

"Yes, I got your little book with the name and number of the little crook. Now, let's get your sorry supposed-to-be-dead ass to Salem before someone bumps into you and has a goddamn heart attack."

Phil laughed, climbed in, and kicked back.

"Do you think I would be less conspicuous if I had a bag over my head?"

"Not less conspicuous, but better looking."

Portland's skyline glistened on Phil's right, I-5 stretched southbound before him, and his past was close behind.

"I'm not breaking any law, you know," remarked Phil as if there was some doubt. "It's no crime to be alive."

Mike nodded.

"It isn't like I'm deserting my wife and kids, either," Phil said as if someone in the car were giving him an argument. No one was giving Phil any argument.

"My wife and I are divorcing, the kids are adults. I'm not leaving anyone with any debts, Mitch will be better off without me, and…"

"And you just want to get the fuck out of Dodge," Mike said, whacking the steering wheel with the palms of his hands.

"Dodge? I want to get the fuck out of the entire state of Kansas!"

Both men laughed.

Gresham and Clackamas were long behind them, when Phil asked Mike a question as if he really wanted an answer.

"Do you think I am doing the right thing?"

"The right thing for who?"

Phil wasn't sure.

"I mean, before I always played it safe. I never ever would have just taken off if I hadn't..."

"Died?"

"Yeah. For some reason that made a difference. I could have walked away any day, driven off into any night, gone to the train yard and jumped a..."

"Waitress?"

"Dammit, Mike, you know..."

"Sure, I know lots of waitresses."

Phil slugged Mike in the shoulder.

"Hey, I'm drivin' here."

Silence.

Past the Canby off-ramp fifteen miles south of Portland, the conversation picked up again.

"Hey, Phil?"

"Yeah?"

"Did you ever read *The Maltese Falcon*?"

"*The Maltese Falcon*? Well, I saw the movie a few times on TV. It had Bogey and what's-his-name, Piper Laurie."

"Peter Lorre, you dumbshit. I saw the movie, too, but did you ever read the book?"

"Naw, why? Did it have hot parts they couldn't put in the film or something? I'm not crazy about smut unless I am experiencing it personally, you know."

"No, not smut, but the Sam Spade detective character tells this story about a guy kind of like you."

"Yeah?" Despite the air-conditioning, Phil cracked open the window.

"Ten years later they find the guy. He's not living faraway at all, and the thing is, this guy was miserable enough to just take off.

And when they find the guy, his life is the same; he's doing the same kind of work and having the same kind of life he did before, so it's ten years later and he's exactly who he was. Only his name and location have changed."

"And what does that mean?"

"People are who they are, I guess. You know, 'Wherever you go, there you are.'" Mike let the sentence hang like a spiderweb. "Where will you be in ten years?"

"Damned if I know, but I am looking forward to finding out." Phil squinted as if attempting to peer into the future. "Costa Rica, India, Africa, Honduras..."

"McNeil Island, Walla Walla, Shelton...," continued Mike, naming well-known Pacific Northwest penal institutions.

"Hey, I am not a crook," intoned Phil in his best imitation of Richard Nixon.

"Yeah, but deep down inside you're a wannabe crook. I always figured the only thing that stood between you and a failed life of crime was your essential stupidity plus a basic lack of creativity and a sincere shortage of guts," Mike teased.

"Gee, thanks," Phil said, growling.

"You start dealing with Mr. Mexico and his import business, and I'm afraid you'll be outclassed by lowlifes," Mike said with a laugh.

"Wait a second, Mike." Phil grew intense but not from anger. "What the hell else am I supposed to do? I have no identification, no social security number, I can't just go out and get a real job here. I have to leave the country to work. I figure it's like taking a nonunion gig. This guy made me an offer of low-risk, decent income, and it may be legal as hell when you get right down to it. It isn't like I am running off to join some goddamn organized crime family. I'm not some Hispanic Marlon fucking Brando, for God's sake. Give me a break. I'm not going to lead some South American revolution, and I don't even speak the language, *amigo*."

"That's a plus," observed Mike sardonically, "because Mexico is in North America. As for your language problem, every person you meet, just say '*hijo de puta*' and smile."

"Heave-ho and punt yourself, smartass. You got any real advice? What else can I do besides pasteurization, construction, and a damn good German accent?" said Phil in a damn good German accent. "Tell me, Sergeant Pepper, can you see any other way?"

Mike knew it was of no use, even by a circuitous route, to attempt to change Phil's mind, so he changed the subject.

"Hey, if they ever make a movie of your life, who plays me?" asked Mike with buoyant enthusiasm.

"Hmmmmm," Phil gave the cinematic casting call serious consideration. "How about Joey Heatherton?"

Mike pretended to lose control of the car.

"We kept on just like that on and off for the hour or so ride to Salem," recalls Champagne, "going back and forth between joking and being serious. I knew I was going to Mexico and that was about it. I wanted a little adventure and a lot less aggravation. Mike gave me two grand in cash, reminded me of his pager number, insisted I keep in touch, and shook my hand. Then I climbed onto the Greyhound heading out of Salem. It was one hell of a long, boring ride. I bought a ticket all the way to Mexico City, but I knew I would have to get off before we crossed the border and do something about ID."

Phil did something about his ID.

"Back when I was a teenager it used to be that you could always dummy-up a fake driver's license from some other state and use it to buy beer or drive a car," explained Champagne. "That was back in the days before cops had all that computerized stuff or driver's licenses had holograms and fancy designs. You could just get some Letraset, a color photo, and with a little work and imagination you could have an ID. Who the hell on the West Coast knew what a real Maryland or Rhode Island driver's license looked like anyway? You just made it up the way you thought it looked."

It had been more than thirty years since Phil had needed a false ID, so it took him a while to recollect the finer points of his creative adolescent endeavors. A Polaroid camera, some smoked glass, rub-on lettering, and three days of trial and error in a bordertown motel room resulted in Phil Champagne entering Mexico with a new name and driver's license to match.

"I called myself Peter Donovan," says Champagne with a shrug, "and the driver's license really didn't look all that great. But it was good enough, because I didn't have any trouble getting across into Mexico and onto a crowded bus to Mexico City."

Whatever romantic illusions Phil Champagne nurtured about a clandestine crossing of Mexico's cordoned borders evaporated in the stifling heat of the overcrowded bus.

"My primary memory of that essentially unpleasant excursion was that every place we stopped, the toilets had overflowed."

He longed for air-conditioned comfort and an ice-cold drink.

Surrounded by strangers speaking an unfamiliar tongue, Phil closed his eyes and pictured himself aboard a powerboat slicing through glasslike water while refreshing spray splashed up from the sides of the bow. Fantasizing his way out of physical and emotional discomfort, he imagined a gentle breeze stirred the treelined shore and that he heard the clink of ice on glass, the splash of a jumping fish, and the sizzle of a thick, juicy steak.

Three

The heaviest baggage for a traveler is an empty purse.
—German Proverb

"Harold Richard Stegeman was a high-rolling restaurateur who sold thick, juicy steaks and drove around Mason County in a fancy Cadillac," recalled *Shelton Journal* reporter Sean Hanlon. "He passed out hundred dollar bills like they were candy and built a brand new business from the ground up."

Terry Kinnaman, kitchen manager at Barb's Country Kitchen from October 1987 until February 1988, insisted that they served up the thickest, juiciest prime rib he had ever seen. Referring to Harold Stegeman, Kinnaman recounted the time his employer took Kinnaman and his wife, Linda, out to dinner at Miguel's restaurant in Tumwater, Washington. Stegeman moved his party to the head of the long line by softly snapping his fingers and slipping the maitre d' a hundred dollar bill.

"I was in awe because I'd never been around a person who

could get other people down before him on their knees like that," Kinnaman said.

Despite the successful grand opening—even Richard Fraley came in three times to sample the menu and offer congratulations—business at Barb's Country Kitchen began to decline. Harold was forced to sink the remainder of the wealth he had acquired for his retirement into the venture to keep it afloat. Good cooks and waitresses were rare in Shelton, and the service declined as the resources dwindled.

Barb placed the final classified advertisement in the *Shelton Journal* in June 1989. The bill for the ad was never paid, forcing the *Shelton Journal*'s bookkeeper, Donna Dooms, to turn Barb's Country Kitchen over for collection. In November 1989, Barb's Country Kitchen and Stegey's Blue Room went out of business.

Harold had borrowed on the restaurant, lost it, and was compelled to sell their home. Next they sold their cars.

Seven separate liens and six tax warrants were placed against Barb's Country Kitchen between April 1989 and December 1990. The unpaid tax bills included $8,923.06 to the Internal Revenue Service, $6,300 to the Washington Department of Revenue, and $573.34 to the Washington Department of Labor and Industries.

Harold Stegeman filed for protection from his creditors under Chapter Eleven of the U.S. Bankruptcy Code, but the case remained unresolved because Harold, Barb, and the kids left town with a travel trailer and debts in excess of $200,000.

"We bought the travel trailer with the intent of moving back to Harold's old stomping grounds in Florida for a fresh start," recalls Barb with a sigh, "but my sister, Mary, fell ill and we went to Post Falls, Idaho, in February 1990 to offer whatever help we could."

They parked their trailer in Mary's yard and stayed for a month or so. Harold Richard Stegeman, a.k.a. Mr. Moneybags, had nothing left except his good name. Harold desperately needed to make money, and that meant taking whatever work was available.

The only work available to Phil Champagne in Mexico was whatever Mr. Smudge Collar's contact could arrange, but first Phil had to arrange accommodations.

"I got off the bus in what must be the world's largest bus terminal," recalls Champagne, "and the cab drivers were crawling all over me."

Vultures picking over freshly delivered carcasses may be a more accurate metaphor. Phil, the bumpkin gringo with no grasp of the language, was fresh meat.

The con ran smoother than the taxi: take the gringo to a third class hotel with first class prices, collect an outrageous fare from the passenger plus an appropriate kickback from the proprietor. If he didn't like the hotel, the driver got a second fare for taking him to another one.

"The first hotel was one step above a dump, and none of the staff could speak any English. It was what a travel brochure would term 'tiny colonial hideaway.' I had already paid the taxi driver, plus I tipped him, and then I had to hire him again to take me somewhere else."

The exchange rate was 159 pesos to the dollar, and Phil's second and acceptable hotel room in the Zona Rosa only set him back a respectable twenty-four dollars.

"And it was not a bad hotel at all," recalls Phil. "They had a first class bar jutting into the lobby off to the left as you walked in the door."

Bars held a certain fascination for Phil Champagne; he had always wanted one of his own.

Comfortably ensconced in his tourist hotel room, Phil Champagne steeled himself to make the phone call. He held the little book in his left hand for several minutes wondering exactly what the first words out of his mouth should be.

The first words should have been in Spanish.

"The person answering the phone didn't speak a word of English, and it didn't seem to matter how many times I said the name of the guy I wanted. I was about to give up when the man I was looking for came on the line."

Champagne had managed, over time and through trauma, to convince himself that his drinking buddy's recommendation would be sufficient reason for a total stranger to embrace him with convivial joviality and a firm offer of employment.

The subsequent chill almost froze the phone line. Phil had to explain, in elaborate detail, how and why he had the man's phone number. At length, the fellow gave Phil another man's name, a number to call, certain code phrases to use, and promptly hung up.

"It wasn't the reception I had anticipated, but as I did get a referral to another number, I was still hopeful."

Call number two yielded more encouragement. Although the contact had at first been reluctant to speak with him, Phil eventually swayed the voice at the other end of the line with his knowledge of prearranged codes. They agreed to meet in the first class bar at the Zona Rosa.

Short, dark, and obviously uncomfortable, Phil's first face-to-face contact contented himself with a cold beer while Phil attempted to make an excellent first impression.

"*Yo no comprendo,*" said the man diffidently as Phil extolled the advantages of having a reliable gringo such as himself on the payroll. "I don't understand what it is you are talking about. You must have me confused with somebody else. However," the man added in an offhand manner, "I know a gentleman in Merida who might help you. Let me give you his name and number. You can tell him I told you to call."

Once again, Phil folded a napkin bearing information and stuffed it in his pocket.

The short, dark man tipped back the longnecked bottle, drained the last of his drink, banged the bottle firmly on the table, arose, and walked out. And just like the smoking beard in the battered blue pickup, he was gone without good-byes.

"Let's get the show on the road," Phil Champagne said to no one in particular and went upstairs to retrieve his belongings before checking out and hailing a taxi to the train depot.

"Before I left the hotel, I asked an English-speaking girl on staff how to say 'train today to Merida,' and she wrote it down for me on a piece of paper. She also wrote down other phrases I might find handy. She spelled them out phonetically so I could pronounce them."

"*Señor, un momento por favor, habla Inglés...,*" Phil tried his halting Spanish on the taxi driver stationed outside the hotel.

"Good afternoon, sir," replied the officious cabbie with mock formality, "my taxi and my command of the language are at your service."

"Now you're talking," said Phil enthusiastically as he hopped in. "To the train depot. I am on my merry way to Merida."

The cab driver shot Phil a bemused glance in the rearview mirror as they pulled out into the crazy Mexico City traffic.

"If you call a thirty-six hour train ride 'merry', you will be very merry indeed."

Phil's merriment dissipated quickly.

"The cabbie took me to the train depot, let me off, and said, 'be careful crossing the street. They will not stop for you.' He was right. I waited for a break in the traffic and ran across the street into a monstrous train station. It was gigantic, but there were hardly any people in it."

After decoding the schedule, Phil walked over to the ticket counter and recited the phrase provided by the girl in the hotel.

"*Merida, hoy.*"

"*No hoy, mañana,*" objected the expressionless ticket master.

"*No, hoy,*" insisted Phil knowing from the posted schedule that there was no reason for him to wait until the next day.

"*Mañana,*" deadpanned the man in the booth.

"*Hoy. Aquí, no amigos. Aquí, no dinero. Merida, amigos y dinero,*" explained Phil, citing neither friend nor money in Mexico City, but both awaiting him in Merida. He played his delivery and facial expression for sympathy. It worked.

"*Qué lastima, lo siento mucho.*" the ticketmaster displayed a gap-toothed grin. "*Merida, hoy,*" he said, and allowed Champagne to purchase a ticket.

The train transporting the former Phil Champagne to the "Paris of the West" was manufactured in England and featured two special cars comprised of nine compartments each; less affluent passengers contented themselves on wooden daybenches.

As Phil was traveling to the cultural capital of the Yucatan, he decided to go first class—he brought along a bottle of vodka.

"I wound up sharing it with a funny little fellow in the compartment across from mine who kept making eyes at me. It turned out that he was eager for conversation in English. He was a representative of John Deere, and the company had offered him a lucrative inducement to master the language. He had a Spanish/English dictionary; I had an English/Spanish dictionary. Between the two books and the bottle of vodka, we made the best of the trip."

Despite somewhat unwieldy urban inconveniences and a tragic history of subjugation and bloodshed, Merida is one of Mexico's most hospitable and nostalgic colonial cities. Following centuries of exploitation as slaves, the Mayans rebelled in the bloody Caste War of the 1840s. It is also Mexico's most important gateway for exploration of Mayan archaeology.

Phil Champagne was interested in neither archaeology nor nostalgia. He wanted an air-conditioned hotel room, and a positive response from his Merida connection.

Once in Merida, Phil boarded a beat-up bus with a blown muffler banging its way down the narrow streets to plop him off near the main plaza. The first hotel to catch Phil's eye was only nine dollars a day with no additional charge for the slowly turning interior fan. No thanks. He opted to pay three times as much up the street for air-conditioning, an English language radio station piped into the room, and a first class bar. No one seemed to mind that this affluent customer paid for everything with cash.

"No one can resist the appeal," says Champagne with a smile, "of a crisp, new hundred dollar bill."

The famous portraits of Benjamin Franklin handed out by Phil Champagne in Mexico were 100 per cent real. The bill tendered by Barbara LeHew Fraley at Señor Froggy's Mexican Restaurant in Spokane on October 15, 1991, was impressive, but fraudulent.

Assistant U.S. Prosecuting Attorney Tim Ohms appreciates a crisp, freshly printed Ben Franklin as much as the next guy, but the next guy wants a real one, too.

"It doesn't matter how pretty the bills look; if they are not real, they are not real. There is more to money than what it looks like or feels like," explains Ohms. "The ink is unique, as is the paper and the intaglio printing process."

Tim Ohms did not always speak with such confidence and unabashed self-assurance on matters regarding Federal Reserve Notes or issues of law and justice.

In the early 1980s, Timothy Ohms was a liberal arts undergraduate devoid of direction. By the joyous yuletide season of 1981, young Tim was in a panic. His college days were rapidly dwindling, and his future loomed as a vacuous financial uncertainty. His college transcripts verified his grasp of Greek literature, but employment prospects for Greek scholars were not among the bold type listings in the Help Wanted section of the *Tacoma News Tribune*. When it came to choosing a career, Timothy Ohms didn't have a clue.

Susan, Tim's older and wiser sister, grew weary of Tim's whining counterpoint to the intended atmosphere of holiday cheer.

"We have a law school right here in downtown Tacoma," growled Susan as only a loving sister can growl. "Be a lawyer and get a life."

Tim was astonished at her suggestion.

"It was like being struck in the head with a hammer," recalls Ohms. "I almost dropped my eggnog. The idea of law school had never occurred to me because I thought you had to do something like prelaw. I came out of a true liberal arts background and had never thought about law. In fact, I don't believe I thought about anything serious at all."

But eight months later in August 1982, Timothy Ohms was attending an orientation class at the Law Center of the University of Puget Sound on Pacific Avenue in downtown Tacoma, right next to the Greyhound bus depot and the dirty book stores.

"I had visions of myself waiting tables at the Old Spaghetti Factory in downtown Seattle and going home at night hunched over a typewriter trying to write, if not the Great American Novel, at least something. So, I went to law school not out of any rational decision, but out of sheer animal panic." Tim shakes his head.

"I had no idea what I was in for. I was neither emotionally nor intellectually prepared for it," admits Ohms. "I was in over my head."

On August 29, 1982, Phillip Wendell Champagne drove through downtown Tacoma, killing time before picking up Larry Wills at the nearby Sea-Tac Airport for the pre-Labor Day Weekend excursion in the San Juans.

"Had I known Tim Ohms back then, I would have parked the car, walked into the University of the Puget Sound Law Center, and invited him along," remarked Champagne. Tim, overwhelmed by the implications of being a law student, would have been too burdened by homework to accept the invitation.

"When I got out of law school, I was still without direction. Things hadn't changed all that much. I still saw myself as Mr. Mediocrity. I jumped at the first job offered to me."

Tim Ohms first job was working at a small law firm in Clarkston, Washington, located in the southeast corner of the state near the Idaho border. In a period of eight months, Tim didn't make a dime for his employers. He was happy to have the job, but hungered for true court experience. When a job opened up as deputy prosecutor, Tim took the position.

"A year and a half after that the superior court judge died, and as there are so few attorneys in Clarkston, one of them was destined to be the new judge."

What Tim witnessed was neither a race nor a wrestling match, but a modified competition not unlike a beauty contest after which then Governor Booth Gardner would award the appointment. The winner was Tim's first boss from the little firm in Clarkston.

Shortly after the shifting of legal chairs and titles, the district court judge retired. Tim's boss in the prosecutor's office became district judge, and the position of Asotin County Prosecutor became vacant. Tim Ohms was the position's interim occupant.

"I thought to myself there is no way on earth that I could, or should, get this as a permanent position. But, what the heck. Stranger things have happened. If I was going to be a lawyer, Asotin County Prosecutor was a job I would love."

In the six weeks prior to the county commissioners' final decision as to who would fill the position, Ohms hardly slept and seldom left the office. He was determined to demonstrate his unflagging determination and tireless dedication.

Only two years out of law school, Timothy Ohms was appointed Asotin County Prosecutor for the duration of the unexpired term or the next general election, whichever came first.

The election came first.

Going from door to door in suit and tie in the sizzling heat of an Asotin August, Tim Ohms campaigned to be elected to the office of Asotin County Prosecutor. He won.

"I figured that no matter what else happened in my life, I would always have this one great highpoint: Asotin County Prosecutor." Despite his attempts at self-depreciation, Ohms did an admirable job for Asotin County. In the early 1990s, his desire for new horizons prompted him to consider moving to China to teach English as a foreign language. A fresh job offer indefinitely delayed an excursion to the Great Wall.

On October 15, 1991, Timothy Ohms assumed his new position in Spokane, Washington, as Assistant U.S. Prosecutor. On his first day at work, Señor Froggy's Mexican Restaurant at 10521 East Sprague, reported receiving a counterfeit Federal Reserve Note in the denomination of one hundred dollars passed by a white female, later identified as Barbara LeHew Fraley.

The bogus bill was identical to those she had passed that same day at Spokane's Pioneer Pies, Frontier West Family Restaurant, and the HiCo convenience store. On November 6, 1991, she used an identical bill to pay for breakfast at Perkins Restaurant in Ritzville, Washington.

"The counterfeit bill passed by Fraley was very unique," commented Secret Service Agent Neil Goodman at the time of Barb's arrest. "It was a 1990 Federal Reserve Note—a new series of U.S. currency just released by the Treasury Department in an attempt to foil counterfeiters. The new bills have a vertical polyester thread between the edge of the bill and the Federal Reserve District Seal. It bears the initials 'USA' and the dollar denomination of the bill." Goodman said the counterfeit one hundred dollar bill seized in Ritzville was a 1990 series, but did not have the polyester thread, which is invisible when the bill is held down on a flat surface. When held up to the light, the polyester thread is visible to the eye.

"This security enhancement," explained Treasury Secretary Nicholas Brady, "was added to one hundred dollar bills and will be added to other denominations because sophisticated color copy machines can duplicate almost exactly older Federal Reserve Notes in circulation."

Linda Bright, the Perkins Restaurant waitress to whom Barb handed the hundred dollar bill, didn't know about the enhanced security or the polyester thread. It never occurred to Mrs. Bright to hold the bill up to the light. If Linda's cash register had been adequately stocked with change, Barb, Harold, and Rich would have never been detained.

"The real irony," remarks Barb, as if it makes any difference, "is that I had no intention of using that hundred."

Could be. She had three other perfectly real ones in her possession at the time. All the other bogus bills were in Harold's pocket.

When Mrs. Bright failed to return, Barb's son, Richard Fraley Jr., became impatient and requested an explanation from a passing employee.

"The manager is having difficulty opening the safe. You will be helped shortly."

Rich offered to hasten the process by paying for breakfast with a smaller bill of his own.

"No, I don't have your ticket handy. Just be patient."

Having been in the restaurant business herself, Barb couldn't believe the poor quality of service.

"I know what it's like to be a waitress," asserts Barb. "I can't imagine how they could justify making us wait so long for our change."

Four

It is suicide to be abroad.

—*Samuel Beckett*

Sitting in the bar at the Zona Rosa in Merida, Phil Champagne, a.k.a. Peter Donovan, found the service and sustenance perfectly acceptable. All he awaited was the arrival of someone obviously looking for him.

The anticipated individual, for reasons purely intuitive, was easily espied. He was in his midthirties, well shaved, medium build and height, nattily attired in a waist-length white cotton shirt with embroidered collar, and he trod on the cuffs of his too-long slacks.

Eye contact confirmed their appointment.

"My first impression was that the guy, Miguel, didn't trust me, and his English was not so hot. I figured I could win him over if I kept at it. In time, he seemed to change his attitude entirely."

First impressions are important.

Donovan recounted his years in the Merchant Marines, highlighted his excursion through the Panama Canal, and regaled Miguel with an animated retelling of the time *Foss LT377* barge, loaded with explosives from Hawaii, "escaped" to roam the mouth of the Columbia River.

To cover all potential employment bases, he put the final punctuation on his verbal resume by listing his accomplishments in the construction trade. Despite his apparent rudimentary grasp of English's more subtle shadings of expression, Mr. Nattily Dressed with the scuffed cuffs stretched his lips and showed his teeth. Peter Donovan interpreted the facial expression as a smile.

"*Comprende* sailboats?" asked Miguel.

"Sure I know sailboats," confirmed Donovan, "I just came from an excursion on a forty-two-foot Westsail." Phil failed to mention that he was presumed drowned.

Miguel examined Peter Donovan as one would a midsize catfish before deciding whether to fillet it and grill it or baste it and bake it.

"Cancun," said Miguel. "You know Cancun?"

Donovan shrugged. He had seen it on the map, knew it was supposed to be Mexico's tourist trap of the future, and heard it was a potential gold mine for builders.

"Miguel said he had a project under construction in Cancun and a sailboat there. He wanted someone to move his sailboat and take on a few other jobs. As he was a man short, he said he figured he had just the thing for a gringo like me. In fact, he said there was another gringo who also recently offered his services. He said we two gringos would be perfect for a few jobs in Cancun."

The mid-1980s building boom that vaulted Cancun into the global tourism arena had yet to ignite, and the Peter Donovan who traveled on Highway 180 from Merida to Cancun through Kantuil, Piste, the ruins at Chichen Itza, Valldolid, X-Can, and Puerto Juarez in Miguel's large, older, American sedan arrived in a relatively small and undiscovered resort bearing only the first scant fruits of preplanned glitz.

The two men checked into separate rooms at an inexpensive hotel in the City of Cancun. Miguel picked up the tab and informed Peter he had two days to play before the job began.

"No trouble," admonished Miguel. "Don't get in trouble."

"*No problemo, amigo,*" said Donovan with a grin, and promptly took off to play tourist.

The city of Cancun was barely beginning to flex its muscle as a raffish boomtown, and the dashing Mr. Donovan was assuredly raffish. He sampled the restaurants and cocktail lounges, made friends with an Israeli businessman, and only moderately unnerved him by singing a German marching song.

"My musical selections were perhaps insensitive, but not ill-intentioned," remember the aforementioned vocalist.

Donovan took a short seabound adventure to Isla Mujeres, a throwback to the days before Cancun ever existed, to explore a ruin of particular interest—the Mudaca Estate.

Fermin Mudaca, Donovan learned, was Isla Mujeres's most notorious pirate. After years of robbing and raiding, Mudaca retired and built a lavish estate to impress a local woman.

"And it still probably wasn't good enough for her," thought Peter, but then realized he may have been reading too much of his own experience into another man's history.

The mansion was in ruins, overrun by the jungle.

"Figures," said the tourist, and he returned to the newer constructions of Cancun.

"Over the next two days, more men came to see Miguel, but I couldn't tell what the hell they were talking about because none of them spoke any English, and Miguel spoke like Pancho on the old *Cisco Kid* show. Finally, he tells me that I'm going to hook up with this other gringo and get to work. I figured it was about time."

The night before "work" was to begin, Phil attended an extravagant tequila party held at a home down a Cancun sidestreet at which he and the other gringo appeared to be the welcome guests of honor.

"The night was a blast. The food was great and there were generous drinks and attractive *señoritas*. It was my first introduction to the other gringo, Sam. He was short and porky with one of those rough, red faces, and he couldn't seem to sit still for five seconds. He was always poppin' up and lookin' around. He reminded me of a hyper Pillsbury Dough Boy. As for the other guys, if they were up to anything crooked, they sure didn't look or act like it. Everyone was as nice as could be."

The following morning Miguel transported the gringos, who were hungover from tequila, down the south coast of the Caribbean Sea not far from Cancun.

A slight distance from a small village, a potholed blacktop road, its edges chipped away and sprouting weeds, gave way to a car-width swath of dirt and gravel trailing past shacks and down toward a concrete dock with concrete bulkhead.

"It was barren and empty looking. All the trees were the same height, about twenty feet, and it was flatter than hell. When we pulled up, there was a van waiting with two guys in it. They didn't get out of the van, say hello, or anything. Considering that there was nothing going on except us, I thought it was peculiar. There were two boats in the water: a good-sized sailboat in front and an older wooden boat behind it."

In addition to the two unmovable strangers in the van, three other men waited in plain sight aboard the old wooden boat. As instructed, Phil and Sam loaded their personal items onto the sailboat, then helped the three men move several weighty wrapped packages from the wood craft to the sailboat. With that bit of manual labor completed, their snappy employer announced that he would pay the two gringos $100,000 to take the sailboat to Marathon, Florida.

Miguel promised to provide them with full instructions and directions. He asked Phil and Sam to wait for a moment on the wooden boat while he went to get them expense money for the trip. The three Hispanics followed along after Miguel.

"Sam seemed pleased and popped on over and sat down at the table aboard the wooden boat, but I was starting to get a giant knot in my stomach. For one thing, smooth Miguel suddenly spoke fluent English, which he sure didn't before. Also, I wondered why the three other Mexicans were tagging along after him if all he was going to do was get us some travel cash and come right back. I took a peek to see what he was doing and where he was going. He went toward the van with the two guys in it, snapped his fingers, and motioned toward us with his thumb."

Mr. Nattily Dressed and his three shadows watched with detached businesslike interest as the two silent men emerged from the van and walked to an advantageous site on the concrete dock. They carried high-powered rifles. Phil Champagne, for the second time in the summer of '82, was in danger of death on the water.

Fear-powered adrenaline pumped violently through his system as he instinctively dove for cover.

"Get down and stay down!" Phil yelled in warning as he hit the floor.

Sam's response was to pop up.

CRACK!

The first shot blew off the side of Sam's head. Subsequent rounds came in rapid succession, blasting into the boat and showering Champagne with wood chips and splinters.

"There were fragments flying everywhere, stuff falling on me and hitting me from all directions. I remember thinking, 'how many in the clip?' 'how long can they shoot?' At least fifty to sixty rounds were fired into that old wooden boat, and there wasn't a damn thing I could do or a place I could go."

Champagne, blessed with an encyclopedic knowledge of firearms, made the parenthetical mental note that his assailants were using more modern weaponry than those with which he was personally familiar.

"I know they were more modern rifles because the high-powered rifles I'm familiar with make a hell of a noise, and these made a cracking noise. I figured they were using Chinese rifles with the super powder. You get almost the same ballistics," explains Champagne, "but without the noise."

Phil imagined that his immediate death was imminent. He only hoped it didn't hurt.

Silence.

"Then I heard doors slammin' and engines revvin' up and I thought, 'Jesus, they're not leaving are they? If I've got a chance to run I better take it.' I got up, and they were going back up the blacktop and coming up this dirt road from the side, off in the direction of the little village, comes this standard, dirty, Mexican p olice car. What they were doing there, I don't know. They weren't really coming too fast. There was a lot of dust and they headed off after the van and the sedan in what seemed to me rather lukewarm pursuit. I could tell that they really didn't want to catch these guys if they were heavily armed with automatic weapons. They were just going through the motions."

Phil looked over at Sam and didn't enjoy what he saw.

"He had fallen sideways and slid under the table. He could have been hit three times for all I know, but I could see shit hanging from the side of his head. As I could see part of his brains, he was obviously dead."

Champagne scrambled from the bullet-riddled boat and boarded the sailboat to retrieve his travel bag.

"I could have grabbed one of those wrapped packages, but I didn't know what the hell was in 'em and I really didn't want anything to do with them. I just grabbed my bag and scooped up about forty or fifty dollars that Sam had in a little box on the sailboat. I knew Miguel and the boys would be back for those packages as soon as they could, assuming those packages were of any value, so I walked as fast as I could up the blacktop to the main road. From there, I could see the top of the hotels. It turned out I wasn't all that far from civilization."

Phil kept up a brisk power walk until he saw a little store by the side of the road.

"I bought a Carta Blanca beer. Later I figured out that it cost me sixteen cents. Then I told the kid in the store I wanted a goddamn taxi. Everyone understands 'taxi.' He got me one to take me into town, then I hailed another one on the street and high-tailed it to the Cancun airport."

The somewhat shaken Peter Donovan wanted the first plane out of town, but the attendant behind the little airport desk didn't speak English.

"Can you believe that? And back then it was a shitty little airport. Jets landed there, but it was still what you would term a shitty little airport."

With frayed nerves and substantial motivation to vanish from Cancun, he began to swear in exasperation.

"A pilot came out from an office down the hall. He had heard me bitching, and he spoke English better than I did. He used my situation as an opportunity to show off. He asked me where I wanted to go, and I asked him what was available. His plane was leaving for Miami in forty minutes. The ticket cost me about seventy bucks, which I thought was reasonable, and despite my previous aversion to airplanes, I wasn't the least bit nervous when we taxied down the runway for takeoff."

Phil Champagne had once wanted adventure, but he didn't want it anymore. Mike was right; he had been outclassed by low-lifes. He had seen one man die that day, and Phil Champagne wanted to just get the hell out of Mexico and never, ever, allow himself to be in a situation like that again. Peter swore he would never again play in Mr. McGregor's garden.

Rising above Cancun, leaving Miguel and a career in import/export behind, Phil Champagne counted his blessings. The first four he thought of were his children. Turning his head away from the aisle, Phil Champagne quietly cried his way to Miami.

Five

Crime is as human as being charitable. Of course, we must have tribal laws. But crime…crime is like art, and the artist has always understood the criminal. The fear of the criminal is the same as the fear of the artist: both are terrified of exposure.

—*Richard Lindner*

Secret Service Special Agent Lyle Workman does not resemble Clint Eastwood, Bruce Willis, or Tommy Lee Jones. Lyle looks more akin to an effervescent Norman Fell topped with a dollop of Tom Arnold. Bouncy, energetic, optimistic, and blessed with a speed racer mind, in the fall of 1991, Workman occupied an office of organized chaos a few floors above Assistant U.S. Prosecutor Timothy Ohms in Spokane's Federal Building.

When Señor Froggy's found that perky employee Jeni O'Neil had innocently accepted a fraudulent one hundred dollar Federal Reserve Note, Lyle Workman got the call. After confirming the falsity of the Note, he attempted to find it in The Secret Service Big Book of Bogus Bills.

The size of a metropolitan telephone directory, The Book lists every known counterfeit Federal Reserve Note passed in or out of the United States. Agent Workman wanted to know where the bill originated, how long the Notes had existed, and whether or not it was an old Note still in circulation or a fairly new one.

The counterfeit note passed at Señor Froggy's was not in the Big Book. Workman called headquarters.

"I wanted to know where it had come up in the United States before, so I asked myself 'Do we have someone traveling through Spokane passing these, or is it the note itself that has made it to Spokane?'"

The answer was neither of the above.

"Bingo!" exclaims Workman. "Lo and behold, they had no record of it either. Since the Secret Service is notified immediately when fraudulent currency is passed, I know the origin is Spokane as of that week. They could be made in Canada; they could be made in Texas, but we know the people who are passing them for the very first time are doing it in Spokane."

In a matter of days, identical notes poured into the Secret Service from Travis Carey at Pioneer Pies, David Davenport at Frontier West Restaurant, and David Nay at HiCo Exxon. O'Neil, Carey, and Davenport unanimously agreed it was a white female with short hair who passed the hundred dollar bills, serial number L44190499E. A notable exception was David Nay, cashier of HiCo Exxon convenience store. Nay remembered receiving the hundred dollar bill, but could not recall a single thing about the person who handed it to him. He did, however, recall absolutely everything about the person on whom he waited after receiving the hundred dollar bill—Sharon Burgerson, an attractive nurse's aide who regularly patronized HiCo Exxon.

The attentive Mr. Nay, perhaps entranced by the customer's selfless dedication to the medical profession, even recalled the sundry nature of the nurse's purchases: a half-case of beer, five lottery tickets, and three packs of M&Ms.

"I have two kids," explained Ms. Burgerson, "so I always grab a couple M&Ms. The third pack was for me."

Strategically placed above the Twinkies, soda, and automotive lubricants, HiCo Exxon has video security cameras. While the recording quality is not broadcast standard, the resolution is often sufficient to identify suspected criminals. If Sharon Burgerson could be found on the videotape clutching a twelve-pack of Busch beer in one hand, and three packs of M&Ms in the other, Nay and

Workman knew that the person preceding her was the passer.

Bingo!

Or almost Bingo.

The videotape revealed a white female with short hair preceding Ms. Burgerson to the cash register and proffering a hundred dollar bill at exactly 5:39 P.M. It also provided a black and white representation of the suspect's clothing, but her facial features were obscured.

"The whole issue was one of identification, not culpability," explains Tim Ohms. "Culpable means blameworthy. There wasn't any real question about her being the culprit, because here was the same individual going to four places in the same area, on the same afternoon, buying a pie with a hundred dollar bill, buying another pie from another store with another identical hundred dollar bill, and so on. It wouldn't be pie in the sky to assume the jury would conclude that this person is culpable. The only real question was 'Who is this person?'"

Barb, Harold, and Richard's $18.73 breakfast at Perkins Restaurant in Ritzville, Washington, on November 6, 1991, suddenly made identification a more complex issue than Workman or Ohms had imagined.

While the young Rich Fraley waxed impatient at Perkins and Barb became increasingly nervous, Harold Stegeman went for a walk.

"I could see trouble coming," acknowledges Stegeman. "I had a stack of counterfeit bills in my pocket, and I knew I had to get rid of them. When I saw Spike's Texaco about two hundred feet away, I figured I had a good excuse to leave Perkins."

Harold Stegeman exited the restaurant and headed for Spike's while Barb and Richard waited for her change. On the way, he stepped over to a ditch and put the bills under a hunk of fresh sod by the telephone booth.

"With a little luck, Barb would appear to be an innocent victim."

Possibly, but it would take luck by the truckload.

"Innocent people do receive and pass counterfeit bills," confirms Tim Ohms, "but they don't behave the way Barbara Fraley did. Even more important than Barb's nervous shaking, for which there could be an innocent medical explanation, was the fact that she left the restaurant without getting back the Note or receiving her change. If you're buying an eighteen-dollar breakfast and leave a hundred dollar bill, that's a pretty good tip."

According to Barb, she only went looking for Harold.

"Out the door I went. The manager, Todd Bright, followed after me with Rich one step behind him. They stopped on the walkway just outside the restaurant, but I continued across the parking lot toward the Texaco."

Barb, suddenly abandoned, was becoming increasingly distraught. She walked around the Texaco, looking in windows for Harold. She couldn't find him anywhere.

"Assuming that she had criminal intent in passing this Note, she picked a lousy place to do it," comments Ohms. "It is one of the busiest Perkins in the world. Todd Bright, the manager, knows what real cash looks like. He recognized it as counterfeit immediately. He had the Note in one hand and the phone in the other when he called the Adams County Sheriff."

Todd Bright not only called the sheriff, he also called Perkins headquarters and reported the situation. He then redialed the sheriff's office to make sure law enforcement was on the way.

"If the Note had turned out to be real, Bright and Perkins would have been very embarrassed, and there might have been legal action against them by Barb. Todd Bright obviously had confidence in his judgment about the Note."

Barb's confidence in Harold as her knight in shining armor was by this time severely shaken. She had violated every rule painstakingly passed down by the all-knowing Harold Stegeman. Knowing he must be furious, she feared he had left her to her own meager devices, mounting panic, and a sense of impending doom.

Named for Phillip Ritz, a hardy homesteader who settled on acreage provided to him by the federal government in 1878, Ritzville is located along a lonely and isolated stretch of freeway that cuts across the high desert from east to west and connects the central and eastern parts of the state with Seattle. In the middle of the desert, Barb felt deserted. When the cops squealed into the parking lot, her extremities trembled with renewed vigor.

"She violated the rules, all right," Stegeman recalls with a laugh. "Rule number one: never pass a bill when you are with the person holding the bundle; rule number two: never cash one when your car is around, or your carrier is nearby; rule number three:

only cash one where it is easy to disappear; and rule number four: never, ever, try to pass a bill in the middle of the desert, especially at a place where they sell pancakes."

Ritzville Police Officer Ken Seuberlich and Adams County's John Hunt arrived in separate vehicles but were a united law enforcement presence for the pancake house scenario. Hunt stayed with Bright and Rich; Seuberlich went to retrieve wandering Barb, who had meandered aimlessly down the road toward a construction site.

Catching up with the ambulatory suspect, Seuberlich asked her what she was doing and where she was going.

Destinations at the I-90 off-ramp are limited, and unless Barb intended to crawl onto the freeway and stick her thumb out, there was no place to go except Spike's Texaco. No one could accuse Barb of attempting to flee—she arrived in her son's Subaru, and Rich was standing right next to Todd Bright the entire time.

"I'm looking for my husband," explained Barb.

"Where was your husband when you last saw him?"

"He was just here with us, but now I can't find him."

According to the authorities, Barbara LeHew Yokum Fraley then said the strangest thing.

"Well, I mean, my husband is at home, but I wish he were here."

Barb had now committed herself to searching for someone who could not be found because he was at home. Not smart; not smart at all.

"That's not what I said," insists an exasperated Barb Fraley. "I said, 'He's here. He was here, but he's not here. I don't know where he's at. My husband was here, but he's not my husband. I mean he's not my husband, but he is my husband. I've lived with him for almost six years, but I'm not married to him.'"

An understandable misunderstanding.

Seuberlich asked to see Barb's driver's license, but her intense shaking made it almost impossible to navigate the wallet out of her purse.

Todd Bright, Rich, and Officer Hunt joined the midstreet discussion. Bright informed Seuberlich that Barb and Rich were two of the three people dining together at Perkins.

"Where is the other man?" asked Seuberlich.

"There were just the two of us," answered Barb.

The breakfast ticket clearly showed three meals; Bright knew three people had been served. Barb, not yet accused of any wrongdoing, appeared to be losing it.

"Nonsense," argues Barb, "I thought they asked me 'How many of you were up at the till.' That's the reason I said that there were only two of us. Then they told me that the hundred dollar bill was counterfeit and asked me where I got it. I told him I got it at Albertsons, the supermarket where I had cashed my check. He asked to see any other bills I had, so I showed them to him and he could see that they were real."

Barb and Rich were placed under arrest, read their rights, and cuffed and stuffed into the back of separate patrol cars. Harold Stegeman watched through the window of Spike's Texaco as Barb and Rich gesticulated in silence, then evaporated in the desert.

Facing the situation head-on, Harold went to Spike's public phone, situated next to the stacked cases of Bud Light and looked up the number of the Adams County Sheriff. Before he could make the call, officers walked through the door.

"I believe I'm the man you're looking for," offered the affable Mr. Stegeman. "I had breakfast with the two people who were just taken away, and I would like to know what exactly is going on."

As always, Harold was the essence of courtesy. He gladly showed them his impressive but fraudulent Cayman Islands resident permit and his authentic Florida driver's license. They took him to the sheriff's office for further questioning.

Lyle Workman didn't meet Harold, Barb, and Rich until 1:45 P.M. Workman was busy conducting another counterfeit currency investigation in Idaho with Coeur d'Alene Police Detective Don Jaran when, at 11:45 A.M., he received a telephone call from Adams County Deputy Sergeant Mike Kline requesting Workman's response to Ritzville in order to determine the genuineness of Barb's one hundred dollar Federal Reserve Note.

"Call the state troopers," replied Workman, "tell them I'm in my car, I've got one lousy blue light, and I am going to be going over the speed limit. I know we can hold the woman until we determine if she did this with intent or not, but the clock is ticking on what we can do with the two guys."

Lyle was also informed that the detained threesome was not being talkative. Barb had already called a lawyer, who advised her to remain silent, sign nothing, and do nothing.

"Right away, I'm thinking that this is the real McCoy. I've got the principals of the case in custody. So I go bustin' butt out there with Special Agent Mick Mikalson. When we arrived, the officers filled us in on the details."

When the Adams County authorities pointed out Barb's cell, Workman walked over for a peek. Had it been a cartoon, his eyes would have sprung from their sockets with his jaw clanging noisily to the floor.

"I see exactly the same clothing on what appears to be the exact lady from the HiCo Exxon video! There is no doubt in my mind that I have the female who passed the Notes a month ago in Spokane. I should have confiscated her clothes as evidence, but didn't. Now I wonder, what else have I got; what else has the net dragged in?"

The net dragged in Harold Richard Stegeman.

"I take one look at this fellow, and he does look classy—blue blazer, khaki slacks, gold chain—and my first mental impression was 'what is this guy doing here from Florida with this nondescript lady who, in my heart, I know is the lady who was in HiCo Exxon passing counterfeit money?' He was very nice, and I believed I detected a slight British accent which only increased my astonishment at him being with these other two. The kid, a real wiseacre, looked like he belonged with Barb. But this guy? I mean, where did this ringer come from? I expected him to explain that he was some distant visiting relative or something."

Harold threw Lyle for a loop. Workman took a good look at Stegeman's identification.

"The Cayman Islands? Florida? Here's this guy who looks like Ronald Coleman, dresses to the nines, charming as possible, and I know he must be behind all this. In my twenty-five years with the Secret Service, I have never encountered a female counterfeit ringleader. I know the kid isn't the brains of the outfit, so that leaves Harold Stegeman. And I know I am going to have to let him and the kid go. Barb I can keep, but those two are simply going to walk away. I know this is the guy, so I gotta be careful what I do with him. I could tell by his beginning comments that he, like Barb and the kid, was committed to not cooperating. They would cooperate as innocent victims of a passing Note, losing their minds, running, all that stuff, but not to the point where they would roll over and tell the truth."

Workman excused himself from Stegeman to speak with Barb.

"I'm not going to talk to anybody until I see an attorney," she stated flatly.

Lyle sat down, leaned over like an old pal, and spoke the truth.

"Here's my problem: I am entitled to fingerprints, photographs, and all other identifying information from any of you because that's a counterfeit hundred dollar bill. I have a right to get that, then I can release anybody that I think I can interview at a later time. You know, Barb, I am definitely not going to be able to release you if you don't cooperate, because you're the one who tendered the bill."

Barb remained steadfast in her refusal to be photographed or fingerprinted.

"You just made it easy," commented Workman, and left the cell to call Timothy Ohms.

"I knew I was going to have to set up an arraignment for her, and in this district you've got to do it as soon as possible."

When Tim Ohms took the call, Lyle Workman began his hyperkinetic retelling of the tale.

"I know right now, Tim, that we gotta bring this lady in. We have to get her arraigned today. I haven't talked to the kid yet, but he did give permission to search his car, which means there is nothing in it. The guy that I'm concerned about is Harold Stegeman. I want to get absolutely everything off his body and copy it. I have every right to know who he is because he was with her. As far as the son goes, we'll wing it."

"I'll start working on the magistrate thing right now," confirmed Ohms. "Call me back if anything changes."

While Special Agent Mikalson searched the suspect's Subaru, Workman took a short run at talking to Rich Jr., whom he appraised as a dedicated wiseacre and wannabe hardass. Richard Fraley Jr., a tall, fine featured and soft-spoken father of twins, admits to an uncooperative attitude.

"Maybe I was supposed to be impressed that Workman had twenty-five years experience with the Secret Service, but to me he was just another cop. I thought Mikalson was easier to deal with."

Lyle, rightly discerning that time spent with Rich was a poor investment, turned his attention to the dapper gentleman from the Cayman Islands.

"Listen, Mr. Stegeman," sighed Lyle, "if you are willing to cooperate, I need photographs and fingerprints. Show me everything that you've got to prove to me that you are who you are and that assures me that I can find you if I need to talk to you again, and you can be on your way. Does that sound okay?"

"Absolutely, Mr. Workman," agreed Harold "I'll do whatever I can to help."

Lyle brought him out to the printing area, and while his prints were taken, the two men engaged in an approximation of relevant small talk.

"He was the nicest guy in the world," says Workman. "I told him that Barb should be much more cooperative, and he said that she had a tough life. I mean, he would make some excuses for her, but not try to fill in what happened, which told me again that he was in control. He was willing to hand her up, willing to let her sit there, but not about to start making up stories about how she got the counterfeit bill."

Harold posed for photographs while Lyle searched his wallet.

"Everything was in place. Then I pulled out a business card from the money part of Stegeman's wallet. Inland Photo Supply. I flipped it over, and BAM! LIGHTNING BOLTS! BELLS! DING-DONG! DING-DONG! THIS IS IT! On the back of the card is the following: arcing light, photo plates, bond paper, opaquing equipment. Here are the ingredients for counterfeiting handwritten on the back of the card. Well, I'm not going to let him see my reaction. Internally I'm going nuts, but on the outside, I don't give it away."

A few moments later, Adams County officers brought Workman a computer printout of the trio's criminal records. Little Rich had one Failure to Appear, Barb had her old forgery charge, and Harold R. Stegeman of 6822 22nd Ave N., Apt 106, St. Petersberg, Florida, was clean as a whistle.

Attached to the short report was a longer, more interesting addendum: the extensive Florida criminal history of Ronald Edsel Kollister, alias Harold Richard Stegeman.

Kollister, a familiar and unpleasant face to the Metro Dade Police Department, was busted on January 19, 1984, for possession of cocaine with intent to sell and placed on probation. Charged with the same offense four months later, he was not prosecuted. The printout read "released to another agency." Two months later, the same play was acted out again. The arrest and release record of Ron Kollister kept a steady pace until his sudden disappearance in late 1985. In America's War on Drugs, Ron Kollister was apparently a double agent.

"Kollister was a real guy, and that was his real name," explains Workman. "He had been arrested and put into the system. I would surmise from the pattern that he may have been working undercover for the DEA. Obviously, at some time in his criminal career, he used the name Harold R. Stegeman. Was our Harold R. Stegeman Ron Kollister? The two men had different social security numbers and different descriptions. I wanted to know who the hell this guy really was, where he came from, and what in the world he was up to."

Despite the identification conundrum and the revelatory contents of Stegeman's wallet, Lyle had no legal reason to hold Harold and Rich. Barb, still refusing to be photographed, stayed behind bars while awaiting transfer to Spokane. The next day, November 7, 1991, the United States of America filed criminal complaint 91-0266A-01 charging Barb with violation of Title Eighteen, United States Code, Section 472.

"I was afraid that I would never see Harold again," admits Barb. "I imagined that he would simply vanish or take off back to Florida."

The thought occurred to him, but Phil never seriously considered it.

"I couldn't turn my back on her like that," insisted Harold. "Besides, I knew it was only a matter of time until they came for me, too. As for Florida, I didn't know what would be waiting for me in Florida."

Phil Champagne breezed his way through United States Customs at the Miami airport, honestly answering "Seattle" as his place of birth.

"It's a good thing I didn't lift any of those packages from the boat in Cancun. After I went through customs, I was asked if I minded being sniffed by a drug dog. The dog sniffed, and I walked away."

A few humid days in Miami's unique sociological atmosphere prompted Champagne to seek another destination.

"Miami is loaded with riffraff in general. There were blacks fighting Hispanics, violence everywhere, and I am just not into that sort of life style, if you can call it a life style."

The image of Sam's brainless head was fresh in his mind, serving as sufficient motivation to jump a bus for Tampa. Once off the Greyhound, Phil Champagne, still calling himself Peter Donovan, checked into an inexpensive downtown hotel within walking distance of the bus depot.

"I think they were going to tear it down, and I bet they have by now. I only stayed there one night, picked up a newspaper, and began looking at apartments for rent. I still had a little bit of money, but it had to be something cheap."

Armed with a newspaper and basic curiosity, Phil Champagne set out to see the sights of daytime Tampa and ended up on a street with no high-rises but "every restaurant known to man on it. Name a chain, one of the links was on this street. I went into a service station and asked if I could toss my travel bag up on one of the shelves while I wandered around, and they were real nice about it. I didn't know what the hell I was doing, or where I was going to wind up. Then I saw the ad in the paper for the guy with the trailer."

The guy with the trailer was an American war veteran with cancer of the larynx who wanted a roommate who might also be his friend. Standing at a restaurant pay phone, Phil Champagne answered all the important questions: "How old are you?" and "Are you gay?"

Phil was momentarily discouraged by the reference to sexual preference.

"No, I'm not gay."

"Good, neither am I."

"How do I get there?"

"I'll come get you."

Despite his recollection of directions and dialogue, Champagne has two handicaps: he is dreadful with names, and he can't spell.

"He had a very common name, but damned if I can recall it. I remember his last name was Polish, but sounded Italian. I do remember that we went out to his mother's house in Brooksville. She had a nice house on the golf course; we stayed overnight and swam in her pool.

"He really wanted to keep me as a buddy because he didn't

have any. Mostly, he wanted to find himself a woman. He knew where they were but was not adept at meeting, greeting, and conquest. It was his idea that we go to a singles' dance. Not as a couple, of course," Phil clarifies, "but in search of women."

With less than a week of Tampa under his belt, Peter Donovan was about to move uptown, alter his life style, and discover he was blessed with a talent far beyond building cost-efficient condominiums. Peter Donovan had a way with women.

High atop a Tampa motel, it was ladies' choice at the singles' dance when he sauntered in the door. Before he could sit down, Peter was dragged willingly onto the dance floor. After five or six minutes of back-beat gyrations, he relaxed with liquid refreshment and romantic implications with dark-haired Ann of forty-seven years, slender build, and swollen bank account. They talked, flirted, and toyed with each other's emotions. He swept her off her feet; she scooped him up and took him home.

A self-supporting woman of sufficient backing, Ann would neither invest her libidinous urges in a one night stand, nor take umbrage at Peter's two-week reluctance at becoming a well-kept man.

"When she first asked me to move in with her, I wouldn't do it. But then I thought 'What the hell, it's better than living with this guy in a trailer court off Elrod Avenue, even if it is air-conditioned.'"

Eight months later, Ann and Peter were still an item.

"I told her that I was a former real estate developer from the West Coast who had lost everything in a messy divorce, which wasn't so far from the truth. Her late husband had been an Air Force colonel who had left one hell of an insurance policy in addition to his military insurance. Her father had died some years before and left her property which she sold for about half a million dollars. She was always buying stocks and bonds and showering me with gifts. The elaborate gifts took a while to get used to, but I adjusted. She had a delightful house just off West Shore Boulevard on the peninsula halfway between Gandy Boulevard and Kennedy Boulevard. I made myself useful by building her a new patio, gazebo, and doing other constructive work around the house."

Not wanting her beau embarrassed by lack of funds, Ann insisted he open his own bank account in which she placed thirty thousand dollars.

"When we started the account, I made sure it was noninterest bearing. That way, I wouldn't have to worry about any problems with taxes, or a double-check of my social security number." While Phil/Peter improved the physical and romantic atmosphere of Ann's domicile, he also improved the quality of his bogus identification.

"The more I made, the better I got at it. I made plenty of it right there in her house, but she never knew. I simply made things that would back up more and more who it was I claimed to be. She was wonderful to me, and I didn't want anything about me to appear suspicious."

As time went by, Ann's gifts became more expensive and increasingly lavish. Phil began feeling both guilty and possessed. He tried refusing her gifts, but that only seemed to offend her.

"Being on the receiving end of a woman's generosity must have been a unique experience for Phil," commented John Robin. "He was always the provider, the one coming up with what it took to take care of things. I can't imagine Phil feeling good about himself in a situation like that."

He didn't, except when he made valid contributions to either the quality of her life, or the size of her bank balance.

During an afternoon visit to Ann's stockbroker, Peter earned her respect as a trusted financial advisor when he rebuked the man for charging her a fee.

"Ann, do you mean to tell me that you're the purchaser of these bonds, and you have to pay him a commission? The seller pays the commission, Ann, not the purchaser. This is bullshit."

The broker's objection never escaped his lips.

"Bullshit," reiterated Mr. Donovan, now turning his attention to the broker. "That's bullshit for you to charge her two per cent on that. Why should she pay you two thousand bucks?"

Rather than appear argumentative, the broker made appropriate adjustments in Ann's favor.

"They do get you on both ends in those deals," notes Champagne, "except if you bitch about it, then they let it go. Well, Ann was real impressed that I bitched. It saved her $2,000 and bought me more than that in credibility and admiration." Ann also bought him a boat. Not a rowboat, not a little powerboat, but a forty-five foot trawler valued at $150,000.

"At first I was furious," says Phil with a shrug, "but, once again,

I accepted the gift. When we finally parted as friends, I went to her lawyer and explained that I still had thirty thousand dollars of hers in my bank account, plus title to this rather extravagant trawler. I didn't want anybody to ever say I stole it or conned her out of it or anything that could get me in trouble. He checked with her on the telephone right there and then. She confirmed that she wanted me to keep the money and the boat. Well, I wrote her a check for the thirty grand and left it with him. The deal was this: if in thirty days she was still refusing to take the check, he would tear it up and the money was mine, free and clear. Thirty days later, he tore up the check."

With thirty thousand dollars in his bank account, and a forty-five foot trawler beneath him, Peter Donovan took off down the inland waterway to the Florida coast via Lake Okeechobee.

"The stupidest damn thing I ever did," insists Phil Champagne, "was trying to navigate those damn canals at night, drunk. Hell, I could have died out there on the water."

Again.

"You don't have to be much of a sailor just to follow the markers and look on your chart."

But Phil lost the markers, couldn't focus on the chart, and found himself in shallow water and high grass in the middle of the night. Champagne turned on his searchlight, scanned the water, and finally discerned the route out.

"Sounds like the story of my life," comments Champagne. "Every time I would get in a situation like that I would pray to God and say, 'I'll never do anything stupid like this again,' and then, sooner or later, I would be right back in the same kind of trouble. Sometimes, like with that damn restaurant, Barb's Country Kitchen, I was too proud to see that I was gonna drown."

Six

My problem lies in reconciling my gross habits with my net income.

—Errol Flynn

Barb and Harold viewed the situation as hopeless. Even when Harold entered severe depression, which was infrequent, he didn't seriously blame anyone except himself.

"I should have known better, but I didn't know anything about the restaurant business. The restaurant was fine; it was the location." Harold suddenly brightened. "Let's blame your sister, Mary."

Barb gave him a look, lit another white-tipped filter cigarette, and tossed the tattered match stick into the motel-style ashtray in the corner of the trailer's imitation kitchen table.

"Good idea, honey. Let's just walk right into Mary and say, 'You know, it's all your fault for talking us into building twenty miles away from where any sane person would go for dinner.' Yes, Mary will certainly appreciate that."

"Hmmmm..." For the first time in a long time, Harold Stegeman was smiling. "Yeah, I'll storm right up to her sickbed, stamp my foot, and yell at 'er about how Shelton is nothing but drug dealers, mushroom pickers, and welfare mothers." Harold and Barb, making light of the absence of such at the end of their interminable tunnel, laughed until tears cued their true emotions.

"You can't get help," said Barb flatly, referring to the incompetence of waitresses.

"You can't get the help to help," added Harold.

"Yeah, the help just brought us down."

"The biggest mistake I made was not shutting down four months after we opened. I should've shut down right then on the spot. I could have said, 'Ooops, let's make this into a house. We'll live in it—anything. But I didn't want to admit defeat, and I kept thinking, 'We'll do this, we'll do that.' Bullshit."

Barb, who had been holding her breath, exhaled.

"We had the customers. We had people sitting on logs outside waiting to get in."

"And the food was good. The prices were right."

"It was thirty-six hundred square feet, and we could have lived in it if we had sold the house. Hell, we could have closed down the restaurant and lived in the damn thing."

The cigarette broke above the filter as Barb stubbed the tip into the ashtray. She shook her head in negative agreement as Harold continued.

"We could have closed the doors and still had $200,000 left over in the bank."

If only, should have, could have—the litany of loss, the chorus of discontent.

Harold and Barb discussed a variety of ventures before building the restaurant. They considered pizza by the slice in the mall, a dry cleaning operation, and several franchise businesses.

"The entire idea," explained Harold, "was for us not to have to work. We make the investment, build it up, hire a good manager, and enjoy ourselves."

It didn't work that way.

"I ended up working six days a week, seven days a week," recalls Barb, "and that got real old, real fast. We took the breakfast shift out and turned the place into a dinner house with lanterns on the table and curtains on the windows. When we first opened up, folks came from near and far for a taste of our prime rib."

They came from as far away as Gresham, Oregon.

Don Robertson, attorney for diverse members of the Champagne clan, stopped by Barb's Country Kitchen with his wife and friends after a weekend of sailing off the Washington coast.

"I'd heard the story about how a former waitress named Barb had a wealthy boyfriend build her this restaurant," explains Robertson. "My friend was showing me around the bar while my wife, Bobbi, waited for our table. I walked in, looked around, and saw a man standing there who looked exactly like my old friend and client, Phil Champagne. As I went to approach him, he turned on his heels and went into a back office. When I returned to Bobbi, she said I looked as if I had seen a ghost. I told her I believed I had."

The apparition may have been Mr. Moneybags to the locals, but he was Mr. Useless around the restaurant.

"I could see that he couldn't tend bar and he couldn't cook or wait tables. He could do dishes, but I needed to have more help than that," says Barb. "So I showed him how to do the books. I had an accountant, but you still have the books, and you still have inventory and things like that. The idea was for Harold to take over the paperwork, so I could concentrate on everything else."

In charge of the books and paying the bills, Harold perceived negative cash flow and financial ruin creeping across the ledger.

"Barb didn't want to face the restaurant's financial difficulties," comments Stegeman. "I tried to tell her many times that the place was going down the tubes, but she didn't want to talk about it. If I started to tell her what was happening financially, she would walk off. I wanted her opinion about what to do, and she said it was up to me. She was working hard night and day to make a go of the restaurant, so I paid the bills in full as long as possible. But when the money wasn't there, I had to decide who got paid first."

Harold made an appointment with the tax people to arrange an extension and devise a new payment schedule. He was promptly advised that he had no right to use collected sales tax for any purpose other than paying sales tax.

"You've got people standing there that need their pay to support their families," protested Harold. "There is not enough to pay both them and the tax. Who am I going to pay first? I'll tell you: I'm going to pay the person who needs the money to feed their family and pay their bills. That's why I'm here trying to work something out with you. Would you rather I paid the taxes and didn't pay my employees?"

No employee of Barb's Country Kitchen ever went home without every cent they had coming; no one who worked for Harold Stegeman could ever say the man didn't take care of them.

Barb may have been tempted to throttle Harold for allowing his ethics to propel them to bankruptcy, but Harold's beloved has a forgiving nature.

"When this happened, I felt like I owed him anyway. In fact, I wanted to make the restaurant work so that I could pay him back for everything he had done for us. I never had to worry about money. He would give me money anytime I wanted it. If one of my kids needed a pair of shoes, he was there to buy it. If one of the boys wanted a car, he would buy him a car. When the younger boy wanted a motor dirt bike, Harold bought him the dirt bike. If I needed something, it was there."

When the payroll taxes needed to be paid, it wasn't there. When the sales tax needed to be paid, it wasn't there. Soon, Harold and Barb were not there either.

Seven

A man who has money may be anxious, depressed, frustrated and unhappy, but one thing he's not and that's broke.
—Brendan Francis

With the ill-fated restaurant reduced to the topic of regretful conversation, Harold and Barb surveyed the future's possibilities from their vantage point of depression. Their future, it appeared, was all used up.

They headed south to visit Barb's sister in Roseburg, Oregon, for a few days, then traveled down to Reno, Nevada, to see her brother who earns his money painting Jackpot Food Marts for Time Oil. A phone conversation with her sister Mary turned Harold and Barb back toward the Northwest.

"Mary was going in for exploratory cancer surgery in Post Falls, Idaho. She was scared and I was worried for her. She asked me to please come and be with her, so I did. We parked our travel trailer in her yard and stayed for about a month before we rented a small house."

Barb found immediate employment at Conoco Port Truck Stop as a cook; Harold bounced from industrial painting to a position as shipping supervisor for Red Label Express. After a year of cooking and shipping, the two were offered positions at a wood manufacturing plant. Harold declined, but Barb accepted.

"I was promised a lot more money than what I was making as a cook. I was told I could make as much as thirty-three thousand a year. I had only been working there a week when I lost half of my little finger in an industrial accident. I was on L&I for nine months and received a small compensation check for the loss of my finger."

The compensation was $720 a month until her hand was healed, followed by a $2,500 final payment.

Harold had all his fingers, but no pies to put them in. The shipping job was employment without destination. Overworked and underpaid, he quit. Stegeman no longer drove a fancy car, nor did he hand out hundred dollar bills like they were candy. Time was not on his side, his head was in his hands, and his beer was lukewarm. So much for being an entrepreneur. It is hard to be a capitalist without capital. Harold Stegeman arrived in Shelton with over $300,000. He had been, in every sense of the word, a self-made man. If self-worth were measured in denominations of negotiable currency, Harold Richard Stegeman had become worthless.

"Becoming a criminal was essentially an executive decision based on financial need," explains Stegeman. "I had to decide exactly what kind of criminal I was going to be. I knew I wasn't going to stick up a bank, because I don't have the guts, and I'm not violent. I refuse to do anything that's gonna hurt an individual. I hate to say this about myself, because nobody believes it, but if I saw a working man drop his wallet and it had $700 in it, I would be the first to see that he got it back. I would not destroy someone under any circumstances."

Harold mentally listed crimes with profit potential, ruling out armed robbery or elaborate cons.

"Never forget," cautions Secret Service Agent Neil Goodman, "that he is a swindler and a convicted felon."

Harold was technically neither when he chose his criminal career.

"Swindler? If I was going to swindle old people, I wouldn't

take their old age money. Now, if an old lady has three hundred thousand in the bank, I might take three thousand of it because that is not going to make a hell of a lot of difference. The idea would be to take a small amount from each person and let it add up. Never take a lot from one person. That should be the rule."

True criminals seldom draft rules of conduct, and Harold hadn't juggled this many justifications since Anacortes in '82.

"Counterfeiting," ruminated Stegeman, "what would that hurt? Even if a shopkeeper dropped a hundred dollars here or there, it wouldn't close him down. And he could probably pass it on to the next person, and they had the option to either turn it in or pass it on. I figured that counterfeiting was the one crime least likely to hurt anybody, and it never entered my mind that I couldn't do it."

Harold began his education with a simple trip to the library in Coeur d'Alene, Idaho. He read a few books; he figured it out.

"I looked up lithography, studied some diagrams, and saw that it was a very simple thing to do. I could give anybody ten hours of instruction and they could do it as well as I did. I figured out my own method, and I went ahead and did it. I was fairly pleased with what I got."

He got twenty-one months.

"The idea was not to counterfeit for a living, but only to generate enough to have a nest egg to start something legit. I didn't realize how difficult it would be to pass enough to have that nest egg."

It is one thing to read about counterfeiting; it is quite another to actually print bogus bills.

"I know a lot of these Secret Service and FBI guys that say that counterfeiting is the last crime you would ever want to get involved in, because every time you cash one, you're sticking your neck out—committing crime after crime, where you eventually gotta get caught."

It was Barb's neck that Stegeman kept sticking out.

"Yeah, well, I do have to take responsibility. But then again," says Harold with an honest smile, "I'm not the one who broke the rules."

Rules are important to authoritarians and game players. "At first it was as easy as a Frontier Pie," quips Harold. "I drove Barb around, and she cashed them one right after another. Somewhere between 4:00 and 5:00 in the afternoon on October 15, we decided to go to Spokane, came down Sprague Street heading west, and stopped at the first business that looked like they could handle it. We just went on right down the line. I remember hitting fast food places and a pie place."

David Davenport of Frontier West Restaurant and Bakery vividly remembered his encounter with the woman who handed him a counterfeit hundred dollar bill sometime after 8:00 P.M. on October 15.

"I told her that our Pie of the Month was strawberry-rhubarb. She said that she would take one, so I boxed it for her. She said that she was sorry, but all she had was a hundred dollar bill. I took the bill and gave her change, and then she left the store. From the time she walked into the building until she left, she was there five minutes at the most."

By the time Davenport realized the bill was bogus, the woman with the strawberry-rhubarb pie was gone.

"I don't like rhubarb," Barb testified ruefully. "I have never liked rhubarb. My kids don't even like rhubarb. I would not purchase a rhubarb pie for any reason."

Lyle Workman always wondered about the pies.

"What did they do with those darn pies? I thought maybe if we had gone out in back of the Frontier Restaurant, or Pioneer Pies, we would have found perfectly good strawberry-rhubarb pies, still in their boxes, tossed in the dumpster."

"No," clarifies Harold Stegeman, "we just tossed all those pies and stuff in the back of the van and kept driving. We cashed twenty-one bills that night. It could have been twenty-two, but I think it was twenty-one, because it was new to us, and we were keeping pretty close track."

Fond memories make for grandiose minimizing. From initial concept to hard currency realization, the project was fraught with failures, falsehoods, and fear. And contrary to early assumptions of the Secret Service, no great thought went into Stegeman's selection of the 1990 Federal Reserve Note as the pattern for his counterfeiting efforts.

"There was no master plan, no flash of creative insight," explains Harold. "In fact, I was sitting in a coffee shop with Barb's nephew, Monte LeHew Jr., when I noticed he had a new looking bill. I asked him if I could borrow it for a day or two. I took a picture of it and gave it back."

As for the security fiber found in real 1990 Federal Reserve Notes, Harold had never heard of it. He knew about the red and blue threads found in authentic currency, but simply chose to ignore them.

"You must remember that I was working with a very small budget on this project, was not using the latest technology, had never attempted this before, and was learning as I went along. After all, if I had been able to go high-tech, I could have afforded to do something legal."

Lyle Workman, well-acquainted with the finest efforts of processional counterfeiters, was amazed at the quality of Harold's barnyard operation.

"What this guy did, the way he approached it, was like something out of the 1930s or 1940s. It was the ultimate in old-fashioned, low-technology, counterfeiting."

"That's me, all right," acknowledges Harold, "old-fashioned and low-technology. I only went to eighth grade, and I have no idea what my IQ is."

Tested in elementary school, he scored ninety-four in the first grade, and eighty-five in the second grade. That was back in the 1930s.

"Forget those old IQ tests," insists Lyle Workman, "there is no doubt that he really is one hell of a bright guy with a remarkable amount of ingenuity. He probably could be anyone he wanted to be if given the opportunity."

On the Florida coast in the 1980s, he wanted to be Peter Donovan, a dapper mariner remembered for his generosity at the bars and his ability to belt out marching songs in impressive German.

"Phil always could do a great German accent," recalls John Robin. "We used to pull that stunt all the time. We would go into cocktail lounges and pretend that we were German tourists or German sailors. I was married to a German girl for quite a while, so I knew the language. Phil just had a natural talent for imitating accents and mannerisms. When he got a few drinks in him, Phil would launch into those German songs. I'm not the least bit surprised to hear that he was doing the same thing wherever he went, whatever name he was using."

At long last, with money in the bank and a beautiful boat of his own, it was a wonderful life.

Phil Champagne had everything he needed, including an excellent set of fraudulent identification.

Eight

How hard it is to escape from places. However carefully one goes they hold you—you leave little bits of yourself fluttering on the fences—little rags and shreds of your very life.
—Katherine Mansfield

The papers authorizing three-year-old Peter Richter to travel unhindered from Czechoslovakia to the British sector of West Berlin in 1947 were forgeries.

"My coat lining and the soles of my shoes contained the few precious stones and what money my parents could call their own," recalls Richter. "My father was in the French underground during the war, joined the British army, and arranged the false papers for mother and I. We were met at the end of the line by two drunk American GIs. I remember that they drove so fast, I could hardly breathe."

Richter and his parents survived Hitler's assault, but his grandmother and aunts were less fortunate.

"My grandmother was Jewish," related Richter, "and when the Germans invaded Czechoslovakia, they started rounding up the

Jews and sending them to the death camps. Grandmother and my father's two sisters were about to embark on a boat for South America when the Nazis came on board. They grabbed my grandmother and one of the girls, but a gentile woman grabbed the other one and insisted that the child was hers. 'She doesn't go with the Jew,' she said. So my grandmother and the one child died in the concentration camp, and the other child was raised in San Paulo, Brazil, by the woman who saved her life."

The Richters left West Germany for America, making their new home in Yakima, Washington. They moved to Lake Oswego, Oregon, in 1950. Graduating in 1962 from the University of Oregon, he decided to take a sentimental journey back to Czechoslovakia.

"When I applied for my visa, I discovered that I was still considered a Czech citizen. It was quite likely that I would be conscripted into the Czech army. Instead of taking the trip, I bought a motorcycle."

Richter passed the Oregon bar in 1971, joined the law firm of Miller, Nash, Wiener, Hager, & Carlson in 1973, and became a partner in 1978. Despite an understandable lack of appreciation for strident German marching songs, he has, as legal counsel for Federal Kemper, been directly linked with the strange case of Phil Champagne since Mitch first filed his claim for the $1.5 million insurance policy.

"My first involvement was June 10, 1983. I received a telephone call from an in-house lawyer for Federal Kemper. Mitch Champagne had filed suit to collect, and this fellow wanted me to take a look at the case. He sent over an Equifax investigative file about eight inches thick."

The agreement and release reached between Federal Kemper Life Assurance Company and William M. Champagne on November 7, 1983, stipulated that $700,000 would be paid to Champagne's attorney, John L. Hilts, who was to deduct his reasonable attorney fees and immediately pay Champagne one-fourth of the balance. The remaining funds were to be held in trust and paid out in fourths, every three months, until the full sum was paid.

The signed agreement specifically stated: "Payment by Company hereunder is expressly conditioned on the assumption that the insured is deceased and claimant agrees that, if at any time, the insured reappears or is found alive, claimant will forthwith reimburse Company all sums paid hereunder, less Hilts' attorney fees." When Phil came back from the dead, Richter was back on the case.

"Once again I received a telephone call from an in-house lawyer for Federal Kemper. They no longer had the paperwork related to the original claim, and their computer only told them that they had paid out $6,000. I advised them that Kemper had paid out a more significant sum."

Kemper filed suit against Mitch, Phil, and little brother John Robin.

"We don't make any claims of fraud against Mitch for two very good reasons: there is no hard evidence of any kind linking Mitch with any attempt to defraud the insurance company; the clear situation with the stipulation in the original settlement which basically says that if Phil ever turned up alive, Mitch would have to pay the money back. Phil is alive; pay us back."

Phil and John Robin, however, are accused by Kemper of conspiring to defraud the insurance company.

"This is not a criminal case, but an insurance matter," clarifies Richter. "Essentially, we are talking about financial obligations."

When news of Kemper's suit reached John Robin, the pain stung as the assault of a serpent.

"First I lost my brother, then Renee accused me of murdering him, then I was sued by Joanne who claimed I was responsible for Phil's death, now they say I helped Phil fake his death so that Mitch could collect the insurance," moaned an incredulous John Robin. "What could I have possibly gained from Phil's death, be it real or otherwise? All I've reaped is anguish, tears, and lawsuits. Why would anyone accuse me of such things?"

Ask Peter Richter.

"Well, it makes sense to seek a default judgment against Phil because he didn't let us know he wasn't dead. The circumstances of Phil's alleged death are such that if Phil faked it, John Robin probably knew about it."

As for what John Robin was supposed to get out of the alleged insurance fraud, Kemper and Richter have no idea. Investigations showed that he had no sudden influx of money following Kemper's payment to Mitch.

A careful check was also made of the financial condition,

credit rating, and recent travel history of Marianne Hauser, a talented and successful real estate agent who had become a close friend of Phil in the months prior to his watery demise. The German-born Hauser, a former ballerina noted for her integrity and business savvy, was the ex-wife of Gresham's Robert L. Hauser. They were divorced on April 30, 1973. The investigation revealed Marianne Hauser had no financial difficulties and an A-one credit rating. If there was a list of likely suspects in a case of potential insurance fraud, Hauser was off the list.

Larry Wills, also subject to careful scrutiny, was on the boat when Phil disappeared, but Federal Kemper made no allegations against him. For the record, Wills's version of what happened August 31, 1982, is the same as John Robin's. When a thorough investigation of Wills's financial situation was conducted on behalf of the insurance company, there was never anything even remotely suspicious uncovered. A primary question Kemper had about Mr. Wills was simply this: "Why had Phillip called him after so long a time to go on a fishing trip?"

It wasn't Phillip who had called, explained Larry, it was Mitch. The two men had lost track of each other for many years after their school days, but their friendship was rekindled in the late 1960s when Mitch tracked him down to repay a $200 debt he had owed Wills for over twenty years. Larry Wills and Mitch Champagne saw each other once or twice a year, every year, ever since. Mitch would go to Boise to hunt with Larry; Larry would go to the Portland area to visit Mitch. As far as Phillip was concerned, he really didn't know him that well. It was only because Mitch had to pull out of the fishing trip that Phil and Larry wound up together.

Larry Wills, of Larry's Carpet and Furniture Cleaning, has never had a complaint against him with the Better Business Bureau, has never been delinquent in his house payments, has never had a tax lien, has never had any financial problems, and has never received any large sum of money that would significantly change his life style. Larry Wills is an honest, hardworking man who enjoys hunting and fishing.

If Larry Wills is telling the truth about what happened the night of August 31, 1982, if Phil Champagne fell overboard exactly as John Robin said, then Phil Champagne is also telling the truth. The possibility makes Peter Richter almost as uncomfortable as when he took Mitch Champagne's deposition.

Mitch wept.

"Either Mitch Champagne is the greatest actor in world, or he never knew that Phil wasn't dead," observed the astute Mr. Richter. "I find it hard to believe that in the ten years that Phil was gone, neither of his brothers ever helped him out. If one of them knew, it was probably John Robin."

Phil Champagne becomes irritated at the very suggestion of wrongdoing on the part of his brothers. "These insurance people are either stupid, crazy, or just plain greedy. They are going after John Robin for no other reason than he is one more person they can chase after looking for a payoff. Hell, John Robin believed I was dead and drowned years ago. He has had more than enough aggravation. They already want a default judgment against me for not being polite enough to let them know I wasn't dead, so why are they going after Mitch and John Robin?"

Seven hundred thousand dollars, Phil, $700,000.

"These characters see everything like it's some big conspiracy," continues Champagne, "and it amazes me. The Secret Service isn't much different. They thought I was some big international crime figure. Then again, they also thought I was that druggie, Ron Kollister."

Ah, yes. Ronald Edsel Kollister, alias Harold Richard Stegeman.

"We thought we were up against some sort of John Dillinger," says Lyle Workman with a hearty laugh, "and it turns out he is just a guy, this character, this sixty-two-year-old runaway from Oregon with a fake name and a real driver's license."

Kollister only attempted to use the Stegeman alias once. On June 7, 1985, he applied for a Florida driver's license in Martin County using Harold's name and date of birth. As Champagne already had a driver's license in that name, Kollister was busted for attempting to do what Phil had already done.

"Serves him right," comments Phil, "first come, first served."

Kollister failed to appear on the charge of using false identification in attempting to obtain a driver's license, and a fugitive charge was issued. The warrant is still outstanding.

"But the money," argues Richter, "how in the world did Phil Champagne wind up in Shelton as Harold Stegeman with all that money? Where did it come from, and how did he get it?"

The answer is Florida, and all because of those damn German marching songs.

"If you're a straight guy; if you aren't gay, Florida is a gold mine of wealthy women," observes Champagne. "What you have is a lot of women, many of them very well off, who have either lost their husbands or are recovering from failed marriages—sometimes several failed marriages. It's not about sex, it's about companionship and friendship. They want someone to talk to, go places, with and share their lives with. And the idea, if you're a man, is to give them your time, your attention, your affection, and never, ever, ask them for money. Let them throw it at you. Oh, you can let them know you could use it, let them know you have things you could do with it, but insist that you would never ask them for it. If they offer it, refuse it…for a while. Then go ahead and take it."

Phil Champagne is not talking about stealing, or if he is, he won't admit it.

"Never, ever, defraud them. Why would you want to do that? If you really have an idea of what to do with it, and you can make them a profit, do it. You're happy; they're happy."

Phil Champagne was one happy Floridian. The old saw of "a girl in every port" was an accurate appraisal of Champagne's life style.

"I admit I probably did hurt some feelings. Maybe some of these women thought I was in love with them or thought they were in love with me. If I hurt them, I regret that. I don't want to live with hurting anybody."

Peter Donovan's trawler became a familiar sight up and down the Florida coast, waves of romance splashing in its wake.

"And they weren't all older matrons," Phil is quick to clarify, "many of them were energetic youngsters with an appreciation of, shall we say, seasoned manhood."

Indeed, the dapper Mr. Donovan's luxury trawler, replete with satellite television reception, full-sized refrigerator, microwave equipped kitchen, and all conceivable amenities, saw many a collegiate overnight visitor. Should the boyfriend of a Ft. Lauderdale lovely become suspicious of his bikini-clad paramour's Spring Break from their postpubescent relationship, Phil would act paternalistically incredulous.

"Do you really believe a man my age would even know what

to do with a young girl like that?" he would ask with an expansive gesture and widened eyes. "More often than not, they would buy it. Sometimes they would become a little jealous when she came back for more."

This was a far cry from the life style in Gresham, Oregon, if what Phil had could by comparison be called a life style. As Peter Donovan, Phil was a man on the move.

"Sometimes I would just go ahead and pay a month's moorage at a time, and more often than not I would find a restaurant with a sea wall. I'd pull in, tie up, and after dinner I would tell them, 'Hey, I'm drinking and everything,' and they would say, 'Okay, just leave it there overnight.' It was no problem. I spent most of my time hopping from moorage to moorage, restaurant to restaurant, party to party, woman to woman. It was like I was on tour."

Having escaped his personal hellhole in Oregon, survived his watery demise in Washington, and reinvented himself as Peter Donovan, Phil Champagne was comfortable enough to dial area code 503. Checking in with Alias Mike, he shared details of his miraculous transformation into a dancing, romancing playboy in the land of sunshine, night life, and generous matrons.

"You were right about Mexico, but I guess I had to learn the hard way. Besides, women are the best adventure."

"Those bastards aren't still after you, are they?" growled Mike. "Because if they are..."

Alias Mike was always eager to act out the more assertive aspects of traditional western male behavior. Military tough and paranoid by design, he traveled America's highways "packin' heat"—a .45 automatic and a Remington shotgun, five in the tube, one in the chamber.

"Naw," laughed Phil, "that was long ago and faraway. My life lately has been nothing but warm weather, cool breezes, and hot women."

In the course of the conversation, Champagne never inquired about his ex-wife, four children, elderly mother, or his two despondent brothers.

"If you can get away on some pretense, come on down and visit me."

Mike found a pretense.

Six weeks later, the two old pals relaxed aboard the trawler in Phil's Ft. Lauderdale moorage. The Florida moon, metaphorically extolled in numerous 1940 Avon mystery paperbacks as resembling a piece of luminous cheese, a dripping mass of silvery opalescence, or a cardboard cutout suspended midheaven by invisible wires, appeared to Phil and Mike as nothing more than a moon. They were entranced by a more immediate and less ethereal example of shimmering translucence—a vodka bottle. Good times, bad times, old times, and lifetimes of little consequence were the topic of conversation. Eventually, Phil asked the question Mike had anticipated. He asked it in a most offhand manner, his eyes averted as if by coincidence instead of design.

"What's going on back home?"

Best as he could, Mike brought him up to date. He related how John Legate was watching Seattle's local television news when the report of Phil's accident came on. John had called Joanne, who in turn called everyone else. Ed Grass heard it from his mother, who had heard it on the radio.

Phil poured himself another drink.

Mike explained about Joanne retaining Don Robertson to launch a suit against John Robin, Mitch's attempts to get Federal Kemper to settle on the Key Man insurance, and the dismal destiny of the ill-fated condominium project which Phil had overseen prior to the San Juan sailing excursion. Mitch never realized a dime from what was known as "Cottonwood." Eagle Mortgage Company of Portland foreclosed, giving Mitch Champagne a guarantee that no subcontractor could bring suit against him. Other than that, Mitch got nothing for his equity. As for realizing a profit, there was never one to realize.

"And," continued Mike, "there was a little matter of alleged insurance fraud."

Phil's grip tightened on the bottle. "Is someone going after Mitch?"

No, someone was going after Renee.

Peter Richter was long gone from Lake Oswego, Oregon, when Renee Champagne began her career as his hometown's premier cocktail waitress. Serving drinks by night and remodeling the former family home on Bel-Air Avenue by day, Renee invested innumerable hours and over $20,000 in improvements to both the interior and exterior of the Clackamas domicile, including new cabinets and floors.

One cold Oregon morning, about 3:00 A.M., Renee returned from work and built a fire in the fireplace before going to bed. A burning log later rolled from the hearth onto the carpet. There were no leaping flames, but there was plenty of smoke; Renee could have died from smoke inhalation. Fortunately, she awoke and survived.

Despite extensive smoke damage and understandable emotional upset, Renee felt assured that the danger had passed. She was wrong. The next day, while Renee was at work, the carpet, which had been secretly smoldering, flared to flames. The resulting blaze spread to the roof, engulfing the home, causing so much damage to the structure that the living room fell into the basement.

Thank god for insurance. Renee contacted family friend, real estate developer and occasional insurance agent, Ed Grass. It was Ed who had held title to the Champagne house and signed it over to Renee after her father's death. It was also Grass, unsuccessful at selling Mitch Champagne a Key Man insurance policy on Phil, who sold Renee a homeowner's policy with Foresters Indemnity. Ed helped Renee file her claim.

"She owned a valuable antique doll collection," recalled Grass, "and I had advised her that we couldn't get it insured without first having it appraised and getting a separate insurance rider. As fate would have it, the doll collection was out being appraised at the time of the fire. Foresters Indemnity accused her of setting the fire herself to collect the insurance after making sure her doll collection would be safe. Don Robertson, the same attorney who represented Joanne in her suit against John Robin, defended Renee."

Ed Grass testified on Renee's behalf, as did the daughter of famed true-crime author Ann Rule, a close friend and co-worker of Renee Champagne.

"Renee was devastated by that dreadful fire," confirmed Rule, "especially coming after the death of her dad. Being accused of insurance fraud was especially insulting, considering how much hard work and effort she had put into that house."

"The jury found in Renee's favor," recounted Robertson. "She emerged vindicated and victorious."

"She was paid about $70,000," recalled Ed Grass, "and she deserved every cent."

Phil didn't realize he had been holding his breath until the excess of carbon dioxide compelled him to exhale. Breathing again, he realized how upset he became at the thought of anything happening to his children.

"That's the hard part, Mike," confessed Phil. "I think about my kids every single day. I wonder where they are, what they're doing, what they're thinking."

"They think you're dead, pal. They think you're dead."

"Yeah. That was the idea, wasn't it?"

"Your idea," said Mike, but not harshly, "your idea."

Phil leaned back and looked out on the Atlantic Ocean. Physical distance is not emotional detachment, and Champagne longed for the best of both shores—his Florida life and his Oregon offspring.

"I've never seen you look healthier or happier," remarked Mike, as if changing the subject or offering Phil another layer of justifications. He was doing neither.

"You can have the best of everything," Mike continued, "but you can't have it both ways."

There it was. Sitting in front of him, big as life, a living, breathing relic and reminder of who he had been and who, in truth, he would always be.

"Remember those damn bikers over in Eastern Oregon that time?" Phil changed the subject. He knew full well Mike remembered those damn bikers. He also had no doubt that those damn bikers remembered Mike.

It was back in about '72 or '73. Phil and Alias Mike were out riding around in Mike's pickup. The two stopped at the Quick Spot convenience store for a fast lunch and a cold drink. When they emerged, seven ruffians on motorbikes decided to play the intimidation game. Off their bikes, the leather clad bullies circled, taunted, and insulted the two men, grabbed their lunches, and tossed them to the pavement.

"Then they decided to screw with the pickup. I knew then Mike was gonna let 'em have it," recalls Phil. "When he reached in and pulled out his shotgun, they stopped in their tracks, but they didn't stop their insults. They backed off some, but they were still acting haughty because they believed he wouldn't kill them in cold blood."

Mike assured the boys he wasn't going to kill them; he was only going to shoot their horses. As the seven men watched in horror, Alias Mike pumped and fired round after round, even pausing to add a few fresh double-aught shells, until every motorcycle was unfit to ride and unsafe at any speed.

"There was gasoline running everywhere, the cycles were shot to hell, and these guys were begging him to stop. Even I was begging him to stop. Mike was always one hell of a shot," asserts Champagne. "When we were younger, we used to shoot silhouette targets. He could drill the eyes right out of 'em. When it came to firearms and accuracy, Mike was just about unbeatable."

The two shared several sun-baked days and balmy nights of nightlife and laughter, usually capped off with several rounds of German songs belted out in Dirty Nelly's, Shooters, or the Marina Inn and Yacht Harbor on S.E. 17th Street.

It could have been one of those nights, or it could have been another. It may have been a similar scene of inebriation inspired musical comedy anywhere along the Florida coast from Fort Pierce to Key Largo, from Shark Point to Siesta Key. Phil says it probably happened in Boca Raton, but it could have been Naples. It doesn't matter where; it only matters that it happened.

A man visiting Florida on business heard a familiar voice singing German songs in a cocktail lounge. A closer look revealed a face as familiar as the voice. The businessman, momentarily taken aback, continued monitoring the musical festivities for several minutes then slid unobtrusively to a pay phone. Had anyone overheard the conversation, the key statement made by the man on the lounge end of the line was simply this: "He is still alive."

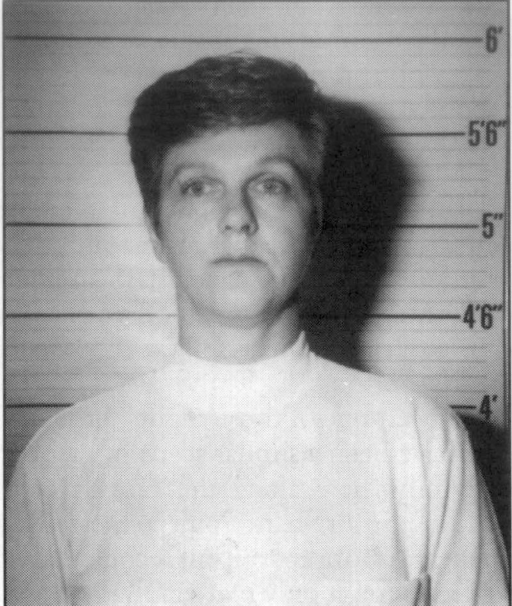

Mug shot of Barb Fraley taken after her arrest at Perkins Pancake House.

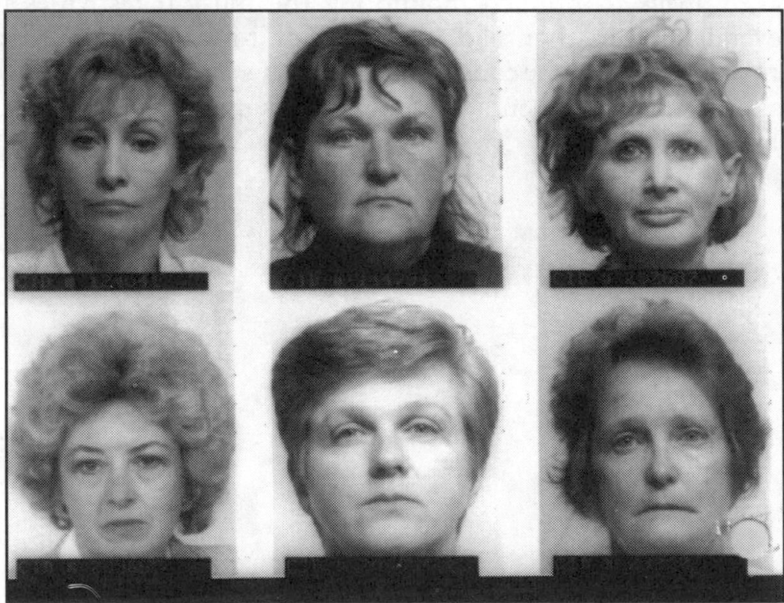

The identification montage criticized during Fraley's trial.

CAYMAN ISLANDS
DRIVER LICENSE

Number	Expirers	Code
4135	6-20-87	1
Birth Date	**Date Issued**	**Type**
6-20-37	6-12-85	A
Height	**Weight**	**Sex**
6' 2"	195	M

Signature
Harold R. Stegeman

GRAND CAYMAN
112

HAROLD RICHARD STEGEMAN
182 KINGS DR. APT. 14
GEORGETOWN

DEPARTMENT OF MOTOR VEHICLES
Director

Phil Champagne's phoney Cayman Islands driver's license in the name of Harold R. Stegeman

FLORIDA
DRIVER LICENSE

OPERATOR 03 85
92
5325-356-37-220 C/F 00 00 00
HAROLD RICHARD STEGEMAN
5822 22 AV NORTH APT 106
ST PETE FL 33710-0000
720
A 6-02 M M 06 20 37
Harold R. Stegeman

Phil's authentic Florida driver's license in the name of Harold R. Stegeman.

United States Secret Service Special Agent Lyle Workman.

Prosecuting Attorney

■ **Responsive to Asotin County**

"Tim Ohms has performed the duties of Asotin County Prosecuting Attorney in a very complete & professional manner. Mr. Ohms' full-time commitment to the Prosecuting Attorney's office has been a tremendous asset to Asotin County."

—Harley Williams, Chairman
Asotin County Board of Commissioners

■ **Responsive to Law Enforcement**

"Tim is refreshing. It's the first time we've had a full-time prosecuting attorney unrestricted by private practice. Tim is responsive—always willing to discuss points of a case, new policies or changes to upgrade the county."

—from an interview with
Sheriff Don Steele, August 1988

■ **Experienced**

The Prosecutor has a unique role as the legal advisor for the county. Tim has over two years' experience in the Asotin County Prosecuting Attorney's Office, and has served as Prosecuting Attorney since January, 1988.

■ **Dedicated**

Tim is the first full-time prosecuting attorney since 1978.

— Democrat —

Paid for by Committee to Retain Tim Ohms, Prosecuting Attorney

Election campaign flyer for Tim Ohms.

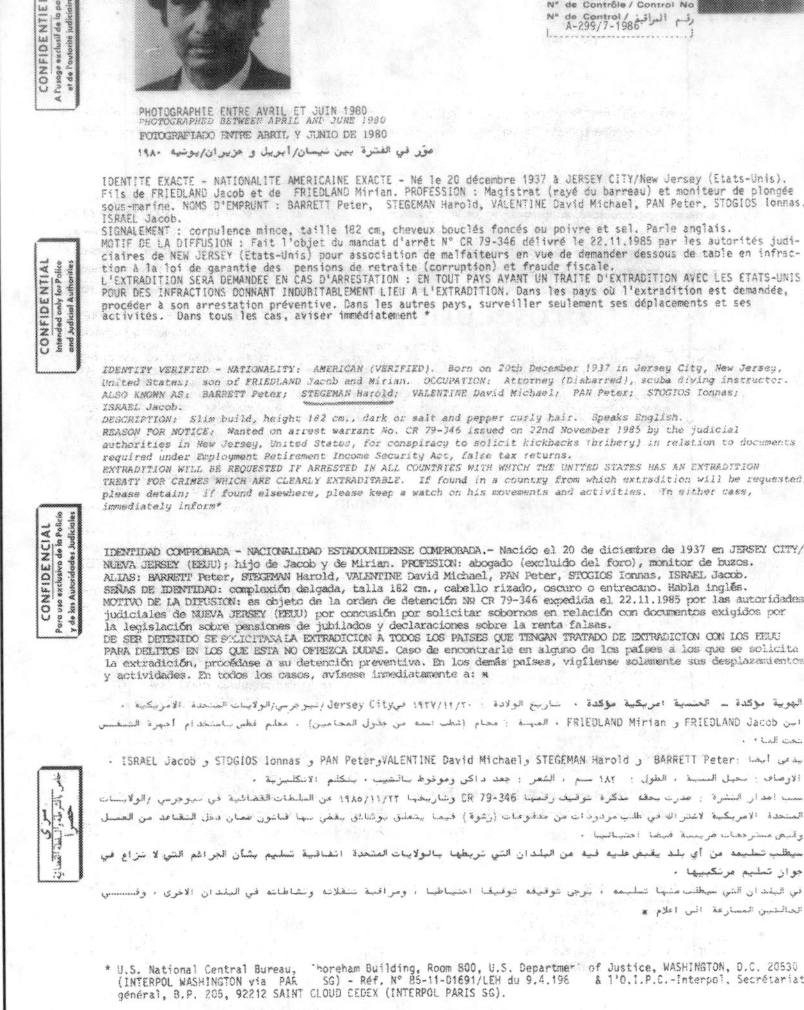

F R I E D L A N D   DAVID JOEL

O.I.P.C. PARIS (SG)
I.C.P.O. PARIS (GS)
أنتربول (الامانة العامة)
N° de Dossier / File No
N° del Expediente / رقم الملف
1318/86
N° de Contrôle / Control No
N° de Control / رقم المراقبة
A-299/7-1986

CONFIDENTIEL
A l'usage exclusif de la police et de l'autorité judiciaire

PHOTOGRAPHIE ENTRE AVRIL ET JUIN 1980
PHOTOGRAPHED BETWEEN APRIL AND JUNE 1980
FOTOGRAFIADO ENTRE ABRIL Y JUNIO DE 1980
صوّر في الفترة بين نيسان/أبريل و حزيران/يونيه ١٩٨٠

IDENTITE EXACTE - NATIONALITE AMERICAINE EXACTE - Né le 20 décembre 1937 à JERSEY CITY/New Jersey (Etats-Unis). Fils de FRIEDLAND Jacob et de FRIEDLAND Mirian. PROFESSION : Magistrat (rayé du barreau) et moniteur de plongée sous-marine. NOMS D'EMPRUNT : BARRETT Peter, STEGEMAN Harold, VALENTINE David Michael, PAN Peter, STOGIOS Ionnas, ISRAEL Jacob.
SIGNALEMENT : corpulence mince, taille 182 cm, cheveux bouclés foncés ou poivre et sel. Parle anglais.
MOTIF DE LA DIFFUSION : Fait l'objet du mandat d'arrêt N° CR 79-346 délivré le 22.11.1985 par les autorités judiciaires de NEW JERSEY (Etats-Unis) pour association de malfaiteurs en vue de demander dessous de table en infraction à la loi de garantie des pensions de retraite (corruption) et fraude fiscale.
L'EXTRADITION SERA DEMANDEE EN CAS D'ARRESTATION : EN TOUT PAYS AYANT UN TRAITE D'EXTRADITION AVEC LES ETATS-UNIS POUR DES INFRACTIONS DONNANT INDUBITABLEMENT LIEU A L'EXTRADITION. Dans les pays où l'extradition est demandée, procéder à son arrestation préventive. Dans les autres pays, surveiller seulement ses déplacements et ses activités. Dans tous les cas, aviser immédiatement *

CONFIDENTIAL
Intended only for Police and Judicial Authorities

IDENTITY VERIFIED - NATIONALITY: AMERICAN (VERIFIED). Born on 20th December 1937 in Jersey City, New Jersey, United States; son of FRIEDLAND Jacob and Mirian. OCCUPATION: Attorney (Disbarred), scuba diving instructor.
ALSO KNOWN AS: BARRETT Peter; STEGEMAN Harold; VALENTINE David Michael; PAN Peter; STOGIOS Ionnas; ISRAEL Jacob.
DESCRIPTION: Slim build, height 182 cm., dark or salt and pepper curly hair. Speaks English.
REASON FOR NOTICE: Wanted on arrest warrant No. CR 79-346 issued on 22nd November 1985 by the judicial authorities in New Jersey, United States, for conspiracy to solicit kickbacks (bribery) in relation to documents required under Employment Retirement Income Security Act, false tax returns.
*EXTRADITION WILL BE REQUESTED IF ARRESTED IN ALL COUNTRIES WITH WHICH THE UNITED STATES HAS AN EXTRADITION TREATY FOR CRIMES WHICH ARE CLEARLY EXTRADITABLE. If found in a country from which extradition will be requested, please detain; if found elsewhere, please keep a watch on his movements and activities. In either case, immediately inform**

CONFIDENCIAL
Para uso exclusivo de la Policía y de las Autoridades Judiciales

IDENTIDAD COMPROBADA - NACIONALIDAD ESTADOUNIDENSE COMPROBADA.- Nacido el 20 de diciembre de 1937 en JERSEY CITY/NUEVA JERSEY (EEUU); hijo de Jacob y de Mirian. PROFESION: abogado (excluido del foro), monitor de buzos.
ALIAS: BARRETT Peter, STEGEMAN Harold, VALENTINE David Michael, PAN Peter, STOGIOS Ionnas, ISRAEL Jacob.
SEÑAS DE IDENTIDAD: complexión delgada, talla 182 cm., cabello rizado, oscuro o entrecano. Habla inglés.
MOTIVO DE LA DIFUSION: es objeto de la orden de detención Nº CR 79-346 expedida el 22.11.1985 por las autoridades judiciales de NUEVA JERSEY (EEUU) por concusión por solicitar sobornos en relación con documentos exigidos por la legislación sobre pensiones de jubilados y declaraciones sobre la renta falsas.
DE SER DETENIDO SE SOLICITARA LA EXTRADICION A TODOS LOS PAISES QUE TENGAN TRATADO DE EXTRADICION CON LOS EEUU PARA DELITOS EN LOS QUE ESTA NO OFREZCA DUDAS. Caso de encontrarle en alguno de los países a los que se solicita la extradición, procédase a su detención preventiva. En los demás países, vigílense solamente sus desplazamientos y actividades. En todos los casos, avísese inmediatamente a: *

الهوية مؤكدة ـ الجنسية امريكية مؤكدة . تاريخ الولادة : ١٩٣٧/١٢/٢٠ في Jersey City /نيوجرسي/الولايات المتحدة الامريكية .
ابن FRIEDLAND Jacob و FRIEDLAND Mirian . المهنة : محام (شطب اسمه من جدول المحامين) . معلم غطس باستخدام أجهزة التنفس تحت الماء .
يدعى أيضا : BARRETT Peter و STEGEMAN Harold و VALENTINE David Michael و PAN Peter و STOGIOS Ionnas و ISRAEL Jacob .
الاوصاف : نحيل البنية ، الطول : ١٨٢ سم ، الشعر : جعد داكن وموخوط بالشيب . يتكلم الانكليزية .
سبب اصدار النشرة : صدرت بحقه مذكرة توقيف رقمها CR 79-346 وتاريخها ١٩٨٥/١١/٢٢ عن السلطات القضائية في نيوجرسي /الولايات المتحدة الامريكية لاشتراكه في طلب مردودات من مدفوعات (رشوة) فيما يتعلق بوثائق يقضي بها قانون ضمان دخل التقاعد من العمل وتقديم مسترجعات ضريبية فيها احتيال .
سيطلب تسليمه من أي بلد يقبض عليه فيه من البلدان التي تربطها بالولايات المتحدة اتفاقية تسليم بشأن الجرائم التي لا نزاع في جواز تسليم مرتكبيها .
في البلدان التي سيطلب منها تسليمه ، يرجى توقيفه توقيفا احتياطيا ، ومراقبة تنقلاته ونشاطاته في البلدان الاخرى ، وفي الحالتين المسارعة الى اعلام *

* U.S. National Central Bureau, Shoreham Building, Room 800, U.S. Department of Justice, WASHINGTON, D.C. 20530 (INTERPOL WASHINGTON via PARIS SG) - Réf. N° 85-11-01691/LEH du 9.4.198 & l'O.I.P.C.-Interpol, Secrétariat général, B.P. 205, 92212 SAINT CLOUD CEDEX (INTERPOL PARIS SG).

Interpol Report on David Joel Friedland, alias Harold Stegeman.

Nine

I know personally several unusually creative photographers who have only a rudimentary understanding of photographic techniques...

—*Andreas Feininger*
The Complete Photographer

On the day of her arrest, Barb Fraley was transported from Ritzville to Spokane by Lyle Workman. They talked about how she was born and brought up on a farm in Wisconsin, and Lyle told her that she looked like a good old Eastern girl.

"I apologized to Mr. Workman for refusing to give him my fingerprints, but I believed I was doing exactly what the lawyer said I should. He said, 'Don't say anything, don't do anything,' so I didn't. If my attorney tells me to do it, then there is no problem."

Lyle, ever the diplomatic investigator, did his best to assure Barb of confirmed legal representation.

"They'll get you an attorney, that's no problem. And I don't want you to talk to me. I don't want you to tell me anything."

Booked into the Spokane County Jail, Barb relinquished her fingerprints. Harold and Rich paid for the impound on Rich's

Subaru and drove home from Ritzville.

"I wanted to go back to the damn phone booth and get the bad money that I hid there, but I was afraid it was a trap," acknowledges Harold. Back in Hayden Lake, Harold reached under his bed for a cardboard box. Inside were sheets of 100 to 150 counterfeit bills which had not been cut out.

"With Rich's help, I burned everything I could think of burning, and still there sat the press. I believed that the law would be there any minute. I didn't want to be seen struggling the press into the van. After all, having a press isn't a crime."

Harold and Rich took all the plates, put gasoline on them, scrapped the images off with steel wool, cut them up into little slivers with scissors, and then put them in a box. Stegeman gave the inks, cleaners, developers, and unused plates to Rich who hid them in the bushes under some old building boards. Harold scrubbed the ink spots off the floor and repainted the big table on which he had worked. He then hooked up his twenty-eight foot Nomad trailer with the van and drove up Highway 95 to Monte LeHew's place at Lake Cocolalla.

"At that time, he lived in a rented trailer on the west side of the highway. I parked the trailer behind his. I told Monte I was in trouble, told him what I had done. He said he knew it anyway the minute I borrowed the hundred dollar bill." After moving the press out to Monte's, Harold stayed up at LeHew's place drinking vodka and fantasizing worst case scenarios.

"I was worried about the counterfeit money hidden by the phone booth because I knew someone would find it, turn it over to the Secret Service, and they would immediately put two and two together. There was only one person in that phone booth with mud on his shoes, and that was me."

Harold Stegeman took another swig of vodka and surveyed his options while eyeing Rich, Monte, and Monte's son, Danny.

"Listen, fellas, I want some of you guys to drive me over there. I'm going to take a chance and try to get the stuff out of the phone booth. I think it's a trap, but what the hell, they're going to find it anyway if they haven't found it already."

It was 3:30 A.M. on the third day after Barb's arrest when Danny LeHew and Richard Fraley Jr. drove Harold to Ritzville in Richard's Subaru.

"Are you sure you can get away with this?" asked a nervous

Richard Fraley Jr. as he slowed to a stop on the freeway.

"Remind me to tell you about my parachute jump in Georgia," Harold answered cryptically, slipping into the grass as the two young men drove away.

The sixty-two-year-old commando crawled flat on his stomach in the dead of a cold November night for about two hundred yards.

"I was about fifty feet from the phone, so I just lay there watching for several minutes. I saw nothing. I jumped up and darted to a spot just behind the phone booth. The money was still there. To me, that meant they were watching, that this was exactly what they were hoping I would do. Then again, maybe they had no idea the money was there, and it would be safe to pick it up. I crossed the freeway and put the bills by a post where I knew I could easily find them again. Then I walked back down through the underpass to the next restaurant down from Perkins and met Danny and Rich. We drove back by the post, picked up the money, and went on back to Monte's place."

The vodka bottle was in Rich's car, and Harold began belting it back once they were on the road. By the time the three characters got back to Monte's, Harold was feeling no pain. He took out the money, now a soaking wet mess, and spread the eighty bogus hundred dollar bills out on the bed to dry. Later, Harold moved part of them off, lay down on the bed, and went to sleep. When he woke up, several bills were missing.

Rich remembers the night of bottled vodka and bogus bills as one of rollicking frivolity.

"We were celebrating having recovered the money from the phone booth, and we were pretty drunk by the time Phil fell asleep. We were playing with the bills, grabbing handfuls of them. I took some, and Monte and Danny probably did, too, but I can only speak for me. As for what I did with the bills, I threw a good amount out the window of my car when I drove through Montana. I was hoping folks would find them and cash them, and that way it would throw the authorities off the trail. The only reason I did that was because I was trying to help my mom."

The bills left on the bed were bundled up by a hungover Harold who wrapped them in plastic and then asked Monte LeHew Sr. to hide them somewhere safe. LeHew cleverly secured the bag under the doghouse.

The following day, Harold and Rich drove the van with the

press to Budget Mini-Storage in Coeur d'Alene. He rented storage unit number thirteen, paid three months' rent in advance, and loaded the space with the press, ink, cleaners, and some unused plates. Stegeman paid cash and told the proprietors that he didn't have his driver's license with him and that he would bring the address later. He said his name was Larry Wills.

No longer trusting Monte LeHew Sr., Harold retrieved the plastic bag from under the doghouse and hid it in the woods temporarily. Later, he took it home to 1123 West Hayden and stashed it in a field.

"I was going to burn it, but at the last minute I decided to keep it and see what would happen. Then I went back in the house and had more time to go through and destroy anything that I thought might be evidence. Somehow, I overlooked that negative they found in my briefcase. I don't remember how it got there. I must have had it with other scraps, numbers that I had cut out to paste in, and things like that. When I cleaned that stuff up and burned it, I simply missed that one little item."

There was another little item Harold missed—Barb. She was released from the Spokane jail on November 14. The only hitch was that Barb and Harold were not officially hitched.

"I don't want you living together," said the probation officer. "You're not married."

"Well, in Idaho, common law is that we are legally married," objected Barb.

"If you can get me a document and prove to me that you are legally married in Idaho, then that's fine. But otherwise, I'm sorry, Harold can't live with you."

Barb looked at Harold and Harold looked at Barb.

"This is where Harold lives," pleaded Barb. "We have lived together for six years. Am I supposed to throw him outside, or am I supposed to go out in the street?"

There was only one reasonable course of action, and Barb immediately suggested it.

"Yes," agreed Harold, "we might as well get married as soon as possible."

There was a significant time constraint involved because Barb was on electronic home monitoring which required her to wear an ankle bracelet that transmitted to a box sitting in the corner of the room. The box connected directly to her home telephone line, keeping authorities continually informed of her movements.

"When they put the monitor on, they give you what's called 'free time.' I had from ten in the morning until three in the afternoon to go as I pleased. It was mainly to seek employment."

They had an hour and a half before her free time was up, yet managed to make it all the way to the courthouse, get a marriage license, hot-foot it to church, and get married. Mr. and Mrs. Harold Stegeman made it home on time. Barb soon found employment as the manager of Spinardo's, a local Italian restaurant, and Harold was hired to do maintenance. Their employer, Glen Mooring, was informed of the charges against Barb. As she was innocent until proven guilty, he had no qualms about hiring a woman with such vast restaurant experience.

"I have worked in restaurants since I was thirteen," confirmed Barb to Tim Ohms during her trial.

"You've been handling money day in and day out since that time," added Ohms. "You must have substantially more experience than Mr. Bright; he's not that old of a person."

"I would imagine I have a lot more experience," Barb asserted, not seeing the intent of Ohms's questions. Perhaps he didn't blindside her, but the jury didn't miss his point: why wouldn't a woman of her experience be even quicker to notice a counterfeit bill than Todd Bright?

"I have never seen any counterfeit money," insisted Barb. "I don't know about markings and all this stuff."

Indeed, Barb steadfastly maintained her wide-eyed innocence up to, through, and after her conviction. Between her arrest and trial were four months of Harold Stegeman waiting for the other shoe to fall.

"I kept expecting them to come for me any day. I kept telling Barb that they were coming for me because I was sure they were going to figure out that I wasn't really Harold Stegeman."

While Harold waited, Lyle worked.

"I had two distinct situations to deal with. The first was helping Tim Ohms prepare the case against Barb; the second was trying to figure out exactly who this Stegeman character really was, and what, if anything, he was up to. We had Harold under surveillance soon after Barb was released and were amazed to find that he was going back into the counterfeiting business."

As it had been a few months since Barb got busted at the pancake house, Harold foolishly assumed he was no longer under investigation.

"I figured that they had not run a check on my fingerprints in the first place and had only kept them for their own records. After all, it wouldn't take that long to identify me if they had my prints. Hell, the FBI should be able to do that in a week or two at most."

The FBI had not been able to do that in three weeks, four, or even more. Workman was checking with Interpol as well, but kept hitting dead ends.

"Maybe because I was broke, I decided to set the press back up and print some more counterfeit money just to have in case I needed it. Of course, I needed a place to do it because it wasn't something I could do around the house."

Harold found a shed on Government Way for only $180 per month. He rented it under the name of Frank Wincheski, a moniker already familiar to the folks at both Spokane's Inland Photo Supply and Litho Development and Research (LDR). According to customer service representative Marilyn Beck, the first time Wincheski did business with LDR was in August 1991. However, it wasn't until Special Agents Workman and Mikalson had shown her a photo of Stegeman that she recalled the incident.

"He said he was working on an invention, but he couldn't tell us what it was because he hadn't taken a patent on it yet. But it had to do with printing plates. He didn't know what kind, size, or even what light source he would be using to burn the plates. He was very vague about the whole thing. I believe we gave him a package of six sample plates just to get rid of him."

At approximately 1:15 P.M., January 6, 1992, Marilyn Beck reported to the Secret Service that Harold Stegeman, alias Frank Wincheski, had just been in her store to purchase a light bulb. She recalled that he had also been in on January 2 to purchase a box of film. Beck noted the car's description and license plate number.

"It was an older, white Fiat station wagon, Idaho plates, #K87781."

A young white male waited for Stegeman in the car.

Barb's kid; Barb's car.

"Barb's kid, Richard, could have got his mother off," remarked Lyle Workman, "if he had been willing to finger Harold and say it was Harold who was behind everything, but he chose not to."

Barb could have freed herself had she been willing to come clean with the Secret Service.

"At no time did I ever think that Barb would tell them anything," insists Stegeman. "I was right. She could have easily told them everything, especially with all the pressure she was under. They would have arrested me and let her go. Every time I think about that, I wonder how I could have been so lucky to have met her in the first place."

Defense attorney Richard Sanger sees things differently, but only slightly.

"Harold could have had the charges against Barb dropped at any time if he had simply stepped up to the plate and confessed to making the bills in the first place. He could have affirmed that she was an innocent pawn in his scheme. He would have gone to jail, but she would have been off the hook. Obviously, Harold wasn't willing to do that."

Harold Stegeman wanted nothing to do with American justice and knew less about its intricacies than he did those of offset printing.

"It took me quite a while to discover that I couldn't print without a printing press," admits Stegeman, shaking his head in combined amusement and dismay. "I actually tried to make a counterfeit bill by printing directly off of the plate. As a matter of fact, I took an eight to ten inch piece of plastic sewer pipe..." Harold stops explaining and starts laughing. "Well, it was obvious that it wouldn't work. I almost gave up on the entire idea until I found I could buy an old Multilith 1250 offset press for $350." Not only were his printing efforts peculiar, his adventures in photography were ludicrously amusing.

"I realized I needed an actual size negative of a bill, but a copy camera was out of the question because I couldn't afford one."

Harold drove to St. Vincent DePaul, a nearby thrift store, where he discovered a whole box of old cameras, and purchased some Polaroid lenses.

"I made a box out of wafer board, about one foot square, drove an inch hole, and held the lens up to it to see if I could get any kind of an image that wasn't totally blurred. It seemed to work. I then screwed the lens on over the hole, caulked around it, and put lights on the other side of it and looked through. It was then that I realized I had to have something to cast the image on. Well, I had read about how they used to use frosted glass in those old portrait cameras. I didn't have any frosted glass and didn't know where to buy it, so I just took a regular piece of glass and put strips of Scotch Magic Tape on it. It looked frosted to me, and it worked just fine."

The film Harold used called for f22 at fifteen seconds with 2,000 watts of light. He didn't know what f22 was, but he figured it didn't really matter. He was right.

Next, he needed a darkroom. Again, Harold used the wafer board and caulking, plus rubber weather stripping.

"I built a box about four-feet by six-feet by four-feet right in the corner of the shed."

When Stegeman explained the Rube Goldberg design of his counterfeiting operation, the Secret Service agents were hard-pressed to keep from laughing.

"He had a Multilith 1250 but never used the machine to its capabilities," remarks Lyle Workman. "In his final printing process, he only printed one image per eight by eleven sheet of paper."

Harold had 500 sheets, and they cost him $18.

"Eighteen dollars is $18, and I didn't have much money. Plus, I figured that 500 sheets with a hundred dollar bill on each one was a lot of loot."

He also had color trouble.

"I ended up with my first batch, less than half of those 500 sheets, printed on a yellow ivory colored paper. It wasn't the right color, and it didn't feel right either. I tried different coloring processes, but I couldn't find any that really worked."

He attempted using water color, but it felt powdery when it dried. Next, Harold mixed yellow and black clothing dye with white watercolor powder.

"I kept mixing and re-mixing until I got a color that looked pretty good. I painted it on with a small brush and let it dry. I did both sides of the bill that way, then I made a cardboard pattern the same size as the bill and cut 'em out with an Exacto knife."

When all was said and done, he was not particularly pleased with the results.

"They looked real bad," admits Harold. "The future batches were much better, but that first batch was real bad, plus I knew there was a flaw in them. But when I showed them to Barb, she said, 'My God, those look good to me.' That was October 15, and so we went on a little drive to Spokane to buy some strawberry-rhubarb pie."

Between the first October passes on Sprague Street and the ill-fated $18.73 November breakfast at Perkins Restaurant, Harold's counterfeiting enterprise went into a second printing.

"This time I went over to a paper supply outfit in Spokane and got some 100 per cent cotton fiber twenty pound bond that had a much better feel to it. I also changed the serial number. When I was done cutting, I had about seventy or eighty bills. I took the ones that were still on the full sheet and put them in a cardboard box under the bed. Then, a few days before we drove to Ritzville, I took Barb to downtown Coeur d'Alene and she cashed five or six of these new bills. One of them we cashed at an auto parts place, two of them were downtown in the new mall, one of them at the liquor store, and the others I don't remember. When a hardware store turned one of the bills down, I said that was enough because we were too close to home and they still didn't look good enough to me."

They also didn't look good to the folks at the liquor store, the mall, or the auto parts store, and that is exactly why Secret Service Agent Workman was in Coeur d'Alene on November 6 when the call came in about the incident at Perkins.

"On the sixth of November we left in Rich's car for the Seattle area without really having an exact destination," recalls Stegeman. "We were just heading for an area that had a heavy business population in an attempt to cash some of the remaining bills, of which I had between sixty and seventy-five."

Barb has a different story. According to her, she was on her way to Olympia to visit her granddaughters.

"I never go out of town or anything without Harold. And my son was going because he wanted to see his kids, too."

"Yeah, that's right," agrees Rich. "We were just gonna go see my kids."

Instead they saw Lyle Workman, and Lyle eventually noticed something peculiar about Barb's fingerprints. There was no print from the little finger of her right hand.

Tim Ohms immediately received an enthusiastic summons to Workman's upstairs office where Lyle thrust the prints under Ohms nose.

"Tell me what ya see, Tim, c'mon tell me what you don't see."

"Slow down, Lyle, you're losing me here."

"No pinky!" Lyle slapped the prints. "No pinky, right? Now,

does that HiCo video show a lady with no pinky? I would love to know."

Ohms and Workman checked the videotape. After being transfered to a still picture and subjected to substantial enhancement, the photo was consistent with someone missing the little finger from their right hand.

"Nobody has said that the person who gave them the counterfeit bill didn't have all their fingers," pointed out defense attorney Richard Sanger. "What they did in this case is determine that the defendant has part of a little finger missing, and then they went back and tried to bootstrap some sort of a nonidentification with regard to a missing little finger out of an enhancement of a surveillance tape that doesn't show anything. I think it is highly prejudicial and doesn't have any relevance to the case."

Ohms pressed the argument, gaining the upper hand.

"The point is that it's consistent with the circumstantial evidence. In a circumstantial case, the government is entitled, under the law, to cast its net out there and bring in what's available."

The net also brought in Harold Stegeman. While the government prepared prosecution, Stegeman prepped his press on Government Way.

"Somewhere around the first of January, I went to the mini-storage place where I had the press, disassembled it into three or four parts so that I could move it by myself and put it in the van along with other paraphernalia. I unloaded it all on Government Way, got some particle board, made a darkroom, made the camera, took the lens and the camera and drilled some holes, put my safe light in and a few odds and ends like that."

On January 10, Harold noticed a "long-haired kook" following him.

"It frightened me because I thought I was under surveillance by the Secret Service."

He was.

"Right then and there, I decided to end the operation once and for all. I went back and took the darkroom down, sawed it up into strips of wood, put it in the van, took it home, and used it for firewood."

Stegeman sold his Multilith press to a hobbyist for $150, cut up plates, and put them in the trash at the Rathdrum, Idaho, garbage dump off Highway 53. He left a note for his landlord saying that he would be gone by the end of the month. Then Frank Wincheski left the keys hanging on a hook and walked away from counterfeiting forever.

"Barbara knew I had been up to something, but I didn't tell her exactly what and we didn't discuss it. She said, 'You're a damn fool.' I have to agree that she was right. No one else had any idea that I was up to it again. The only bills I had left were the ones I took from under Monte LeHew's doghouse. I put them in a raisin box on a shelf on the porch until I could decide what to do with them. Hell, I should have burned them right away because, after all, they weren't real."

According to Detective Inspector Brian Gibbs of the Royal Cayman Police Department, neither was Stegeman's Cayman Islands driver's license nor his residence permit.

"Both documents are bogus," declared Gibbs on May 11, 1992. "The driver's license number, 4135, has actually been assigned to someone other than Stegeman since 1975. Further, the address given for Stegeman on both documents, 182 Kings Drive, apartment 14, Georgetown, is not good. There is no such street as Kings Drive in Georgetown."

Detective Gibbs offered another enticing tidbit of information—the name Stegeman had been used for travel purposes by international criminals.

Interpol confirmed that Harold Richard Stegeman entered Costa Rica from Miami on January 12, 1985, using Costa Rica permit #399219, and returned to Miami the following day. While Interpol was unable to explain how the person using the Stegeman identification could make this international travel without use of a U.S. passport, they were able to report that an identical trip of one day's duration was made to Costa Rica from Miami by former New Jersey Senate Minority Leader David Joel Friedland. Glib, charismatic, and touted as New Jersey's future governor, Friedland graduated from Rutgers University to enviable positions in both state politics and private legal practice.

In the late 1970s he was indicted and convicted for taking loan kickbacks. Friedland arranged for con artist Barry Marlin to receive a $4 million loan from the Teamsters, taking $360,000 for himself. The senator was also charged with jury tampering and tax evasion. Convicted in 1980, Friedland appealed his conviction and began cooperating with the FBI, helping them gain convictions against other corrupt officials. At the same time Friedland was helping the FBI catch the bad guys, he was preparing a $20 million double-edged rip-off of the Teamsters' Union.

The wily ex-senator arranged for the $20 million to be invested in Omni Funding, a mortgage company which he secretly controlled. The Teamsters believed Omni was lending on low-risk, FHA approved projects at an interest rate of ten per cent. In reality, Omni lent the $20 million to high-risk ventures piloted by entrepreneurs unable to achieve funding elsewhere. For the honor of Omni financing, the borrowers paid twenty per cent instead of ten per cent.

According to U.S. Department of Labor Special Agent, Tom Sommero, Friedland also extracted kickbacks and partial ownerships in a variety of ventures, including a coal mine in Kentucky, a restaurant in Palm Beach, and bingo in the Dominican Republic.

As the ventures went belly-up, Friedland and his criminal cohorts turned their ill-gotten personal profits of $4-6 Million into South African Krugerrand and Canadian Maple Leaf gold coins. Loaded with gold and anticipating indictments, Friedland devised a clever ruse. On Labor Day Weekend, 1985, shortly after the third anniversary of Phil Champagne's tragic boating accident of Lopez Island, David Joel Friedland faked his death in a scuba diving accident off the Bahamas. Again, the Coast Guard received a frantic call. Friedland was missing and presumed drowned.

Unlike Phil Champagne, Friedland didn't stay dead long. He resurfaced in London, granted press interviews, and contacted old cronies to shake them down for cash. Displeased with Friedland's tactics, his indebted associates preferred to disclose his whereabouts to Special Agent Sommero rather than pay the former senator.

"We tracked Friedland through Kenya, Rome, and Hong Kong," confirmed Tom Sommero, "and finally to the primarily Moslem Maldive Islands off the West Coast of India. These are resort islands frequented by European and Japanese tourists and famed for scuba diving. As Friedland is an expert scuba diver, he loved it there. He also devised numerous schemes involving local investors, one of whom became suspicious and reported him to the authorities."

The reason for suspicion was the name on his passport—Richard Smith Harley—a name regretfully similar to that of a British mercenary remembered for arranging firearm shipments from Sri Lanka which were used in a failed coup attempt. Intolerant of such behavior, island authorities detained Friedland for ten days, during which time they attempted to ascertain his true identity. On the seventh day, they perused the latest Interpol Red Alert, recognized his face, and contacted the U.S. Department of Labor.

"On Christmas Day, 1987, I arrived in Male on the Maldive Islands," recalls Agent Sommero. "When Friedland walked into the room and saw me, he immediately turned to his captors, professed his belief in Islam, and begged for asylum. He insisted that his life had been threatened by Khadafi of Libya!"

No asylum was granted; no extradition agreement existed between the Maldive Islands and the United States. No matter. The unwelcome scuba diver was unceremoniously stuffed into Agent Sommero's departing plane. Imprisoned at the Fort Dix New Jersey Federal Correction Facility, David Joel Friedland no longer uses his home in North Miami Beach, his condo in the Bahamas, his lawyer in the Cayman Islands, or his false United States passport in the name of Harold Stegeman.

On October 31, 1985, sixty days after Friedland faked his death in the Bahamas, Harold Stegeman applied for a United States passport. This Stegeman was not David Joel Friedland. He was also not Ronald Edsel Kollister. He was Phil Champagne.

Ten

Any new system is worth trying when your luck is bad.
—Heywood Broun

Don Robertson has sincere affection for at least one of the three Champagne brothers.

"Phil Champagne has always been a dear friend and valued client," remarks Robertson, "and in all the years I have known Phil, both before his tragic accident and after his reappearance, I have never known him to lie to me about anything."

Robertson is not as close to John Robin—it was Robertson who represented Joanne Champagne in the wrongful death claim against him—but their friction is not enough to ignite sparks of anger nor prompt one to speak too ill of the other.

"Robertson and I had somewhat of a falling-out back in about 1977," explains John Robin. "I tried to take him to court over a project he got me involved in. Strange as it may sound, in the long run it worked out well for me. I wound up paying about three hundred thousand for some property, and sold it for six hundred forty thousand. Robertson may have been miffed that I wanted to take him to court, or perhaps," says John Robin with a laugh, "he was irritated that I came out of the deal making such a nice profit."

While Robertson endorsed the brothers' version of what happened over the long weekend in 1982, there are others who suspect that the three brothers conspired to defraud Federal Kemper. Such cynics see conspiracy in every action, no matter how trivial.

"It seems a bit much," offered one of such persuasion, "that Phil, Larry, and John made such a spectacle of themselves at Boomer's Landing in Anacortes with the waitress and all that. Maybe they just did it to corroborate their story."

If such were the trio's intentions, they were ill-founded. Interviewed by insurance investigators on February 23, 1983, Boomer's Landing employees Linda Carlsen and Priscilla Lemphuir had no recollection of any group of three men being served on the night of the accident, nor did they recall waving good-bye to anyone from the window. The women emphasized that the restaurant was busy, and just because they couldn't recall the men or the incident didn't mean it didn't happen.

Conspiracy?

The concept of conspiracy implies that the participants are of like mind, share a common foundation, are united in their views and thoughts, and that their purposes are in harmony.

"John and Mitch didn't speak to each other for five years," noted mutual friend Ed Grass, "and all because they disagreed on how to do foundations."

John and Phil were close.

Phil and Mitch were close.

John and Mitch had nothing to do with each other.

"I was the first one to become a builder," says John Robin, "and then Mitch and Phil came into it, too. We worked together for a while, but that was years ago. Phil and I would set up jobs and scout property, and it was Mitch's position to supervise construction. He would make mistakes in pouring the foundation, and it ended up costing us twice as much as it should. I guess the thing that really made us break up the corporation was one particular incident, one particular foundation. The cost overruns for that foundation alone were about fifteen hundred dollars because Mitch and his foreman were pouring the walls thicker than they needed to be."

Displeased with the expensive foundation, Phil and John told Mitch how to set up the next job.

"It was ridiculous to throw the money away like that, so he agreed and said he understood," recalls John. "But I'll be damned if on the next job he'd gone and done exactly the same thing. When I confronted him about it, he said, 'Well, you build things the way you want, I build them the way I want.' I told him that the money he was spending was partly mine and that we had made a mutual decision as to how it should be done and it was his job to do it that way."

This conflict ended the Champagne brothers' triumvirate of cooperation. Mitch was about to marry his new wife, Dorothy, and she didn't think Mitch should take orders from his little brother. The assets of the corporation were divided. Mitch took five houses; Phil and John took the rest.

Mitch and John didn't speak, but Phil maintained positive relations with both. Not long before Phil's accident, John Robin took the initiative to patch things up.

"I went to where they were building and talked to him. I told him I thought it was ridiculous that we didn't speak to each other. After all, we're brothers. We might have some differences, but that is no reason to not even talk to each other. He agreed, so we shook hands and I felt better about it. We didn't ever become close, but at least we spoke once in a while."

Would John conspire with Phil to defraud Federal Kemper on Mitch's behalf?

"I didn't even know about Mitch having that insurance on Phil until Renee made allegations that I murdered her dad. She told the authorities that I was more an enemy than an uncle. I found this out from the state police when I had to go make a report about what happened. When I heard about the million-dollar policy I thought, 'Oh, great. I lost a brother, his family is suing me, and now Mitch has got a million-dollar policy. The insurance people are going to be sure that brothers, a situation like ours, they're gonna figure...'"

They figured. Perhaps Mitch and Phil conspired to defraud Federal Kemper, but left little brother John in the darkness of self-recrimination for the past ten years.

"There is no hard evidence that Mitch Champagne conspired to defraud the insurance company," reiterates Peter Richter. "No such charges have been, or will be, made."

Phil Champagne shakes his head in amazement.

"See how crazy it gets? John and Mitch weren't that close, and if you knew Mitch you would know that he has never, ever, done anything wrong. He is the most law-abiding, conservative fellow on God's earth. I keep telling people that it was all my fault, all my choice, all my desire to get the hell out and start a new life. Even if I was near broke, it was better than what I was going through in Clackamas. Maybe if I had never left Florida, never come to Shelton, never made counterfeit bills, or maybe if Barb had used a real bill for that damn breakfast, no one would ever know that Phil Champagne was alive."

"I think he wanted his kids to know he was alive," remarks Barb. "It was tearing him up inside to not see his kids. I think a lot of what we went through was the result of Phil wanting his kids to find out that he was alive. He can't even think about them without getting all misty."

The mere mention of Kathy, Renee, Curtis, or Phil Jr. sends their father into wet-eyed reveries.

"When Ann gave me that beautiful trawler in Tampa and I had it moored over by Waring's Marina, I wished the kids could see it, enjoy it, and spend time with me on it. But I knew that was impossible. Every time I did something new and adventurous, I wanted to tell them about it, share it with them, see the look in their eyes."

Phil begins chuckling to keep from crying.

"If you ask the kids, they'll tell you I never liked to fly. In fact, it used to be a major trauma just trying to get me on an airplane. But when I was hanging out in Ft. Lauderdale I even learned to sky-dive. I only jumped twice. Once at the airport with some folks I'd becomes friends with, and the other time in Georgia."

Formerly a man who never took chances, the resurrected Phil Champagne became fearless and daring.

"I figured since I had already died, what could possibly happen to me? When these new friends of mine in Ft. Lauderdale suggested I jump out of an airplane, I decided to go for it. I didn't much care for it, but it turned out to be a valuable experience in more ways than one. First of all, I learned I could do a simple static line jump. Second, I met a private pilot by the name of Stretch who was probably about as shady as I was, and more adventurous. We became occasional drinking buddies, and I had a standing invitation to drop by his place—a trailer near the airport—anytime I wanted. But then again, I always did have a knack for making friends."

Gregarious, outgoing, and courteous, Phil Champagne by any other name was still a man well met by those who met him. A delightful conversationalist, he was forever expanding his circle of well-to-do friends and ne'er-do-well sea-going associates. Marinas, cocktail lounges, and Florida social occasions were all conduits of connection for the charming Mr. Peter Donovan.

"I used some other names too, or to be precise, I had identification in other names. You might say I became mildly addicted to having several sets of false identification. If something went wrong, I could always be somebody else."

Something went wrong, terribly wrong.

"Would Mr. and Mrs. Champagne mind if we fictionalized this story?"

The question comes from Patricia Brown, cohort and consort of television producer Anthony Spinner. They make made-for-television movies, a genre with specific requirements.

"Television movies are female driven," explains Brown. "We are looking for women's stories, told from a woman's perspective, with a strong female lead."

Elizabeth Montgomery, Valerie Bertinelli.

"Would they mind if we made Barb's brother a cop or a private eye? You see, we're thinking that maybe it would be interesting if it was Barb who unraveled the secret of Harold's true identity. She is innocent, of course. First she has counterfeit bills, then a counterfeit husband. Now she must embark on a journey in which she searches for truth—the truth about the man she loves, and the truth about herself."

Really?

Phillip Krupp of Zev Braun Pictures, one of America's more successful high-profile producers of television programming and motion pictures, has no interest in fiction; he wants facts.

"I have a moral obligation," explains Krupp, "to make sure this story is true before I attempt to sell it to a network. If I were going to fictionalize it, why bother buying the rights? I could make up my own story if I was interested in fiction. If this is true, I want it proven to me so that I feel comfortable with it."

Phil Champagne has no argument with either approach.

"I don't care if they make me a cartoon mouse," says Phil. "And they can make Barb a leather-clad secret agent working undercover at a restaurant, brandishing a spatula in one hand and a .45 automatic in the other if it makes them happy. But since this is a true story, and it is crazier than anything anybody could cook up, why don't they just tell it like it is? If they want proof, I'll give them proof. What proof do they want? Would they like Ann's exact address? The name of her lawyer? The only thing I will not reveal is the exact location of the dead bodies."

The dead bodies come before the Georgia parachute, and both come after Mike's first visit.

"Mike had actually flown to Florida in a private plane belonging to a relative of a former wife. He had cooked up some business reason why the guy couldn't come with him once they were in Ft. Lauderdale," explained Phil, "and Mike had to rejoin him later that night. Of course, once that ex-relative reads this book, he'll know exactly what was going on."

What was going on was vodka, conversation, and camaraderie. Mike and Phil arranged elaborate methods of renewed communication—letters to prearranged mail drops in different names, and cryptic messages culled from the pages of Moby Dick.

"It was kind of like a game or a puzzle. I would get a letter at the mail drop saying something like 'chapter five, paragraph two.' I would go to the library and look it up. Perhaps it was childish, but we both got a kick out of it."

Before Mike left, Phil shared the secret of trawler access.

"In case you come back sometime and I'm not around, here's how you get into the boat."

"Ah," observed Mike, "the famous Florida keys."

In mid-July 1985, Peter Donovan sailed southwest from Ft. Lauderdale past Key Biscayne, Key Largo, Plantation Key, Upper and Lower Matecumbe Keys, Long Key, Duck Key, and Boot Key by Marathon, and anchored slightly southwest of Spanish Harbor Key on the edge of Looe Key National Marine Sanctuary.

"I took two couples out. I believe they were all county employees I had met at a local watering hole. There was Leonard Spain, John Bullard, Marie Nelson, and Rosie somebody—I forget her last name. They were diving in forty feet or less, and I was doing my usual thing: sitting up on the blind bridge having a drink, looking toward shore."

Fewer than 500 yards west sat an Italian made aluminum boat, close to 100 feet in length.

"It was an older model," recalls Champagne, "so he probably paid $1 million or $1.5 million for it. A new model costs about $6 million. You couldn't help but notice this one right off; it was bigger than most of the other boats anchored in the area."

Phil saw a human speck bobbing and waving far from the Italian craft.

"Jesus," thought Champagne, "that guy is too far away. Even if he dumps his tanks and tries swimming against a half a knot current, he's gonna be exhausted and not make it. It's way better than 300 yards."

Phil picked up his marine radio and tried contacting the ship. No response. He tried again. Nothing.

"Hey," shouted Phil to Leonard and John, "I'm going to go play hero and save this guy."

Grabbing the inflatable, eight-foot, U-shaped Zodiac, Champagne sped through the serene Atlantic and pulled the man out. Dazed, desperate, clutching, and thankful, the gasping and gulping gentleman explained that he had indeed run out of both air and energy.

"I didn't check his tanks to see if he was really out of air or not, I just gave him a hand. He looked totally exhausted to me and seemed madder than hell that his own folks hadn't noticed that he was in trouble. He kept going on and on about how I saved his life. What happened to him was not unusual. I know because I scuba dive. You can go under and be quite surprised when you come up exactly how far away you really are."

Forty-five days later, David Joel Friedland would experience the same problem off the Bahamas.

Returned to his own ship, the recovering diver launched a tirade *en Español* against those who had failed to notice his predicament.

"You must stay for a drink," insisted the rejuvenated victim, introducing Phil to a number of individuals whose names he would never recall.

"You saved my life; I am indebted to you forever. You're my brother, that is the Cuban way."

Phil knew nothing of "the Cuban way," but knew everything about accepting hospitality. He shared a drink with his new "brother," a fifty-year-old gentleman calling himself Raul Medina.

"He wanted to know all about me, where I moored my boat—he even took pictures of it—and asked me all sorts of questions. I guess I stayed aboard about an hour. I tried calling over to my trawler, but nobody answered. This Medina character kept telling me that I was his friend for life, but I figured his enthusiasm would wear off soon enough."

It didn't.

Four days later, a long white limo pulled into Phil's Ft. Lauderdale moorage. Out stepped Raul Medina, with a woman of exceptional beauty and intrinsic allure.

"This is my sister," explained Raul.

Phil didn't care if it was his sister, his aunt, or a casual acquaintance. A dark-haired beauty with big dark eyes, 5' 7", with "petite, unobtrusive breasts," Esperanza Medina attracted Phil's attention and activated his latent libidinous impulses.

"We have come to invite you to a party Friday night at my home in Boca Raton," exulted the gregarious Raul as Esperanza's eye contact proffered intimations of possible party favors.

Invitation accepted.

"There is a lot of money in Boca Raton, and much of it was invested in Medina's home. While not right on the water, it was close enough. It was a lovely place with attractive architecture and a well-manicured lawn. There must have been forty or fifty people there, and the party spread from the lawn into the house. There were folks shooting pool, and some car dealer who did a lot of television commercials was there. He damn near talked my ear off, but the party seemed perfectly normal. Raul was a charming host, introducing me to all these people. He seemed quite genuine, and Esperanza followed me around giving me that 'wait till I get my hands on you' look. All in all, it was a delightful affair."

The affair between Phil and Esperanza was launched two days later.

"She showed up alone at the moorage explaining that she

wanted a better look at my boat," says Phil with a laugh. "I knew better than that."

Phil gave her the guided tour; she returned the favor. Two nights later, Esperanza decided she needed a change of clothes. She drove back to Raul's with Phil, where any objections to her overnight antics remained undisclosed.

"I became a semipermanent fixture around the place," remembers Champagne. "I swam in Raul's pool, ate Raul's food, and made love to Raul's sister. The only problem was that he kept asking me what I did for a living, how long I had been retired, all that stuff. I forget the details of my impromptu recitation, but basically it was a reiteration of the 'retired builder from the Bay Area' story."

One August afternoon, Raul took Phil into the den for a little heart to heart. Champagne feared it was about Esperanza, but instead it was about gratitude.

"I owe you my life," began Raul, "and I haven't forgotten it. It is only right that I do something to repay you, at least in part."

Phil's courteous attempts to alter Raul's tone met with firm resistance and the offer of vodka.

"I have something in mind," continued Raul, pouring inebriation over ice, "something that could make you a good amount of money. But it isn't something I can discuss in detail. I will tell you this much: I want you to do something for me, and it is not something difficult. If you do this, I will give you $200,000."

Phil listened with renewed acuity.

"Before we discuss this further, I want you to come with me to my ranch up north, be my guest for a few days. You'll have everything you could want," Raul paused for a nod and a smile, "everything except Esperanza. Can you handle that, my friend?"

"*Ja wohl*," intoned Peter Donovan, stamping his foot.

Raul tossed back his head, laughed aloud, and slapped Phil on the shoulder.

"I love it when you do the German," exclaimed Medina, and he meant it.

Eleven

All men should strive to learn before they die,
What they are running to, and from, and why.
—*James Thurber*

Departing from Boca Raton's private airstrip the next day, the men flew far north, refueled midstate, and transferred to a helicopter somewhere over the border.

"We followed the river, taking the curve, then we set down in a large open area surrounded by what I call 'scrub pine,'" remembers Champagne. "You wouldn't exactly call his place a ranch or a farm—it didn't have livestock—but it did have plenty of pine trees, bushes, and a well-built, recently remodeled split-level home.

"It was an older building, but well preserved. I remember that the roof was Dutch gable with tile. But it was flat tile, not Mexican tile. It had a long, long driveway that went right into a big two-car garage. You couldn't go directly into the house; you had to open the door and go across the breezeway into the kitchen. It had a full basement with a rec room. No pool table, but a bar. It had kind of a restaurant look to it. There was a lot of dark wood and what I call European paneling—the kind with raised surfaces. It had French doors and windows with leaded, beveled glass. It was obvious money had been spent on the place."

The isolated location was not devoid of inhabitants. In addition to the two hyperkinetic Dobermans, ten men awaited Raul's arrival.

"They all spoke Spanish, and a few of them spoke no English whatsoever. I was introduced to all of them, but I wasn't sure why. I just tagged along after Raul and he showered me with hospitality—food, drink, and a comfortable, relaxed atmosphere."

The atmosphere turned to isolation when Raul talked business with his Hispanic entourage. Phil, the obvious outsider, was placated with an unending supply of vodka.

"Raul still hadn't told me exactly what he was up to, or what it was he wanted me to do. The next thing I knew, I was left alone with the dogs and the caretaker."

Apologizing profusely, Raul explained that a sudden business matter required his attention. Phil was to stay at the ranch until his return.

"Now look," said Raul, "I'll be back as soon as I can. Draw your own conclusions, but I've got something I have to take care of, and I can't run you all the way back. You may be a bit lonely, but the caretaker will cook you anything you want, or you can cook it yourself. Consider this your own home," Raul offered graciously.

Phil didn't have his own home. He had his own boat, a floating habitat financed by a former flame, but "home" was an idealized illusion from his painful past.

Not wanting to offend his host or allow $200,000 to elude his grasp, Phil responded with polite assurances and self-deprecating humor.

"Go ahead and do what you gotta do. After all, if you wanted to kill me I'd be dead by now."

Raul found the remark very amusing, gave Phil a manly hug, and took off with his entourage.

"I was left with those two dogs who were not too adept at conversation. It was monologue by me and tailwagging by them. Raul and the gang were gone a day or two, and a couple more guys showed up before he came back. They didn't speak English and were very surprised to find me there. I didn't know them; they didn't know me. We just nodded at each other and wondered what the hell was going on."

Cordoned off by lack of communication, Champagne ensconced himself on Raul's patio for relaxation and another round from the never empty vodka bottle. From the kitchen's AM radio, immune from the shading effect of hills and trees, came an old Elvis tune.

"To the King," intoned Phil to the surrounding scrub pine, "who's been dead even longer than I."

Phil never had a thing for Elvis. The only connection between the peripatetic identity shifter Phil had become and the swivel-hipped icon of rock-'n'-roll was the 1962 Seattle World's Fair. Elvis utilized the Northwest locale for the cinematic musical comedy *It Happened at the World's Fair*. Phil's older daughter, Kathy, became paralyzed while she was there over the summer vacation.

Accompanied by her maternal grandmother, Kathy took in the sights, sounds, tastes, and experiences of what was a singularly exciting event in the otherwise uneventful summer of '62. She rode to the top of the Space Needle, compared the speed of futuristic touch-tone telephones to the standard rotary dial models, eyed with suspicion the Communist Russians acting officious in the Soviet Union exposition, and sampled the hard brown bread, open-faced sandwiches advertised as "The Danish Delight."

Her back ached; her legs felt weak. Perhaps it was all the walking. The discomfort increased; her ability to control her legs decreased with alarming rapidity.

Assured by a local doctor that there was nothing wrong with her that a couple of aspirin couldn't cure, Kathy took the tablets and retired to bed. However, instead of gaining strength, she began losing control of her legs, then lost all sensation.

Her father immediately took her to another physician who, at first, believed the young girl had polio. Phil knew full well that Kathy had been vaccinated and proved it to the doctor. Tests. More tests. Kathy's lower extremity sensations were soon limited to her big toe. After continued investigation, the culprit behind her creeping paralysis was found to be a spinal cyst growing between her shoulder blades.

Surgery and physical therapy put the bounce back in her step.

Within weeks, it was as if it never happened. Phil never forgot it.

Elvis's Golden Oldie segued into the Four Tops' "I Can't Help Myself"; Phil Champagne stood, stretched, and continued the interminable task of waiting for Raul.

"He returned jubilant, energetic, and radiating friendship. He was like a fresh summer breeze, warm and buddy-buddy-like as ever. Raul appeared as pleased to find me still there as I was to see him get back. To tell the truth, I was bored to tears."

There were only two ways out of Raul's country estate: helicopter or highway. Phil was a welcome guest, but five land-locked days of canine conversations and hand signals with strangers was not Champagne's idea of a rustic vacation. He kept reminding himself of why he had been invited. Money. Lots of money. Phil found that the contemplation of significant amounts of money was an excellent antidote to boredom.

At long last, Raul ushered Phil into his dark paneled study. Sitting behind his large desk, Raul scratched his chin and seemed to be in doubt as to where he should begin. He swiveled his chair around and pressed on a panel which popped open revealing a brown banker's box. Raul retrieved it, placing it on the desk.

"It wasn't a secret panel, nothing mysterious about it, and the box was as plain as can be. But the cash—now that was impressive."

Raul smiled as Phil eyeballed the fresh bills.

"Two hundred thousand dollars, my friend, and I promise you that it is all yours for doing what will be a very simple and enjoyable task."

Champagne attempted to appear relaxed and confident, but the two preceding days of infinite boredom had him leaping inside like a pup welcoming his master.

"You do a remarkable German accent, Peter," began Raul, leaning back in his chair, "and that makes you perfect for what I have in mind. You see, there is a boat sitting in the Cayman Islands. German registry. It is a simple matter. The German owner must appear with the appropriate papers to have the boat released. Simple. I will provide you with everything you need—the papers, a crew, as they say, 'the works.' All you do is be a convincing German. Show up, sign the papers, and have a pleasant boat ride back from Grand Cayman to Tampa. We will be waiting for you, bring you back, and this money is yours. Well?"

It sounded simple. Not too simple, but simple enough. There

was obviously something off-kilter about the enterprise, but Phil Champagne knew he was not being paid $200,000 to ask questions.

"They won't release the boat to a Cuban," added Raul, referring to himself, "or to a Mexican or to a Panamanian. German ownership is what the papers say, so a German it must be."

Phil nodded as if it all made sense. Perhaps it did; perhaps it didn't. The money, however, made perfect sense, and in his mind, Champagne was already spending it.

"Any German in particular?" asked Champagne in an offhand manner. Damned if he was going to appear to be an ingrate.

"Yes, your name is Klaus Kruger. That is the name on the papers."

"What about identification?" asked Phil as if forged papers were something unique and wondrous.

"Identification that appears to be authentic is not difficult to produce. We'll take some pictures and, well, it is a small matter with which you need not be concerned."

"I understand," said Champagne, and he certainly did.

Raul smiled and picked up a pen. Ripping a slip of paper from his desktop notepad, he spoke as he wrote.

"This money is for my gringo friend, Peter Donovan, to whom I owe my life."

The note went into the box, the box went into the wall, and within the week, Phil and Raul went to the Cayman Islands.

"A few days before we took off, we went to Raul's house and took some pictures—passport photos—and I did some signatures. It wasn't long before they had an authentic-looking German passport and some other vessel documents in German which I couldn't read. We left from the Miami airport, and I was sober. I know that because I still am not crazy about flying if I'm sober, so I wasn't in a very good mood."

Adding to Phil's discomfort, his travel companions conversed in Spanish for the flight's duration.

"There were about six of us that went to Grand Cayman," recounts Champagne, "Raul, the guy that he was always with, who I don't believe spoke any English, and these other guys who I didn't know. No women. I don't know what the hell they were talking about. Every once in a while Raul would apologize to me for not keeping up a conversation I could follow. Under the circumstances, it all seemed normal."

Landing in Grand Cayman, Phil was transported to a hotel where he was introduced to the Norwegian captain who would bring the boat back to Florida.

"Then we all just screwed around, had dinner, and didn't discuss anything much at all. The next day some fellow Raul knew on the island, a lawyer or something, took us down to the docks. Everyone was laid back, relaxed, but businesslike. I didn't have to go in and demand my boat, or really do much of anything. It didn't bother me a bit to do this; I wasn't nervous at all. I had my part down to perfection."

Klaus Kruger said his lines, waved his papers, signed a book, and identified the Norwegian as the captain of his ship.

There was the small matter of a fine, but another glance showed that it had been paid in full. No problems. No problems at all.

Raul didn't accompany Phil aboard the ship, but planned to fly back to Ft. Lauderdale.

"You guys get on your way," advised Raul. "I'll arrange transportation for you from Tampa and meet you at the house."

Phil, the Norwegian, and four others piled into a small boat on the docks, fired it up, and headed on out to get the ship underway. They traveled without incident around the western tip of Cuba and headed for Florida.

"The vessel was originally built as a whaler. It was 100 feet, steel, with Mercedes diesel engines. It was a beauty."

Phil Champagne, alias Peter Donovan and Klaus Kruger, was a happy man.

"This is the easiest money I have ever made in my life," thought Phil. "I'll do this act as many times as they want."

Slicing through the open water, Phil Champagne felt oddly free. Perhaps it was the exhilaration of having performed so perfectly; perhaps it was anticipation of the $200,000. It may also have been the personal pride of knowing he had pleased his pal Raul.

Phil watched the ship's captain pour himself another cup of thick, black coffee.

"We have a saying in Norway," said the captain with the most dour of expressions, "it doesn't take a lot of water to make a good cup of coffee."

It looked more like wet tar than fresh java.

"Bet you can eat that stuff with a spoon," commented Phil, still doing his German. The captain didn't laugh; he only nodded. "Raul must have really wanted this boat," continued Champagne, dispensing with the Germanic intonations, "and I can't blame him. It's a beauty, isn't it?"

The captain laughed and took a noisy slurp from his steaming mug.

"You better believe it. What's even more beautiful is the money he's getting for what's in the hull."

Phil forced a smile.

"Yeah? What's in the hull?"

The stocky Norwegian raised his eyebrows, and Champagne suddenly had memories of himself desperately searching for markers in Lake Okeechobee.

"If you really don't know," remarked the captain as if Champagne knew everything, "all I can say is, 'Welcome to Crime on the High Seas.'"

Twelve

Truth is not a matter of opinion. Truth may be investigated and ascertained.

—Buddha

On March 4, 1992, the United States State Department Diplomatic Security Division Special Agent Bob Kircher reported to Lyle Workman that a person using the identity of Harold Stegeman had made application for and received a U.S. passport on October 31, 1985, in Tampa, Florida.

On March 5, 1992, State Department Special Agent Mike Hudspeth obtained certified copies of both a birth certificate and death certificate in the name of Harold Richard Stegeman. Hudspeth confirmed that the real Harold Stegeman died November 4, 1945, in Dade County, Florida, at the age of eight. He immediately faxed this information to Lyle Workman at the Spokane office.

On March 6, 1992, three days before Barb's trial was to begin, an arrest warrant was prepared for Harold Richard Stegeman, a.k.a. John Doe, for one count of conspiracy to pass U.S. Obligations.

"Barb and I were working at Spinardo's Italian Restaurant, getting the place ready to open. There were painters and carpet layers waiting for us when we got there," relates Harold. "We pulled up in our van ready to go in, unlock, and do the usual stuff. Suddenly, Workman's buddy [Special Agent Mikalson] whipped in driving a Blazer, and pulled around as if he was trying to block me. I couldn't figure out what this long-haired, goofy-looking guy was up to. He jumped out, pointed a gun across the hood of his Blazer and started yelling, 'Get up against the wall! Don't move; I'll shoot.'"

Mikalson did not arrive alone. Perhaps fearing that an unarmed sixty-two-year-old man and a diminutive waitress might try to intimidate him, several four-wheeled law enforcement vehicles pulled up to lend needed emotional support.

"Don't you dare pull a weapon!" Harold was warned.

"Check her purse, she might have a gun in there!"

If Harold Stegeman had not been on the receiving end of such noisy indignities, he may have found them amusing.

"First the deputy sheriff has me up against the wall, then I get the handcuffs, and then I gotta get in the Sheriff's car. The deputy asks me if I have any weapons on me or anything that I could use to hurt him."

Harold closes his eyes, shakes his head, and laughs the soft laugh of experience and forgiveness.

"He's got an old man handcuffed, and I'm supposed to pull a weapon on him?"

While Harold was cuffed and stuffed, Barb was dazed and confused.

"They didn't tell her anything; they didn't even tell me why I was being arrested. It was all guns and screaming and barking orders. My God, what a bunch of Boy Scouts. I only had time to tell Barb one thing—I told her to get rid of the bills in the raisin box on the front porch."

Unflappable as ever, the cooperative Mr. Stegeman assured his captors that he posed no threat to their safety.

Barb's pleading eyes searched for Harold in the back of the sheriff's car. He gave her a smile and a memorable parting comment.

"It makes me lose all respect for law enforcement officers when they act like this."

Lyle Workman awaited Harold's arrival at the Kootenai County Jail. He didn't know who Harold was, but he knew who Harold wasn't.

"We Mirandized him and he verbally waived his right to an attorney at that time," recalled Workman. "During preparation of a Personal History Summary, he provided information still using the name Harold Richard Stegeman."

Harold confirmed that he had resided in Hayden Lake, Idaho, with Barb and two of her children, Jerry Fraley, age sixteen, and Leanna Fraley, age thirteen, since 1990. He told them about living in Shelton from 1986 to 1989. Harold was honest when he told them he lived in Florida from 1984 until 1986, although he falsely placed his residence in St. Petersburg.

"From 1949 until 1984 Stegeman said he resided in the Cayman Islands with a man he believed to be his uncle, but 'wasn't sure whether he was an uncle or not,' Frank Lattimer," says Lyle Workman. "When we asked him why he did not ask questions about his parents and why he was placed with this friend/uncle, he indicated, 'I never asked Frank Lattimer about my family. He wasn't the kind of guy who talked much.' From 1937 until 1949 he supposedly resided in Miami, Florida, with Lattimer, who he claimed was deceased."

When Harold was done reciting the fabricated history of his life, Workman let him know the jig was up.

"We know you're not Harold Stegeman. The real Harold Stegeman died at the age of eight. The U.S. State Department is preparing a warrant for the use of this false identification in preparation for an application for the passport you received in October of '85."

If Workman expected Harold to become unnerved in the face of this shattering revelation, his expectations were in vain.

"He made it clear that he was not the least bit concerned about such charges as false identification, driver's license, and such because they would only result in minor fines or insignificant sentences. He did speak of wanting to help his wife, whose trial was about to start, but thought it would be best to contact an attorney for what he termed 'advice on other issues and events in his life.' As always, Harold, or whoever he was, was a true gentleman."

Now that Workman and Stegeman both knew Stegeman wasn't Stegeman, the obvious question was: "Who is he? Really?"

"I'd love to tell you everything, fellas, I really would," said the affable Mr. Stegeman, "but I think I'd better talk to a lawyer first. I might wind up doing time, but if I do, it won't be because of involvement with the Secret Service."

Workman and Mikalson were more baffled than ever.

"For all we knew, we were dealing with an international criminal, possibly the mastermind of any manner of nefarious undertakings."

The United States of America vs. Barbara Ellen Fraley went before the Honorable Fred L. Van Sickle on Monday, March 9, 1992. Timothy Ohms represented the United States of America; Richard Sanger represented Barb, Harold Stegeman's new bride.

"This is a criminal case," explained Judge Van Sickle to the jury, reviewing some of the basic rules. "First, the defendant is presumed innocent until proven guilty. The indictment brought by the government against the defendant is only an accusation and it is nothing more. It is not proof of guilt or anything else. The defendant, therefore, starts with a clean slate."

The arrest of Harold Stegeman also wiped clean a significant portion of defense attorney Sanger's approach to the case.

"Do you really think it was a coincidence that they arrested Harold immediately before the trial was to begin?" asks an understandably cynical Sanger, "or was it a coincidence that the government did a highly publicized search of the Stegeman home on the last day of the trial, the same day that Barb testified on her own behalf, the day before the jury went into deliberations?"

Sanger did not find the supposedly innocent synchronicity any more amusing than he did the photo montage of possible suspects shown to witnesses at the trial.

"All of the witnesses said the person who passed the counterfeit bill in their particular business had short hair. The government investigators picked up on that and put together a photo montage in which they placed only one person with short hair: Barb."

When Lyle Workman took the stand, Sanger hammered him about the montage.

"Is it an accident, Agent Workman, that in the montage Barbara Fraley's picture is larger than the pictures of the other ladies in the montage?"

"Yes, it is. I cannot explain that," answered Workman.

"And is it an accident, Agent Workman, that Barbara Fraley's picture appears in the center of the montage?"

"Entirely."

Sanger portrayed Barb as the sandbagged fall guy for a government unwilling to pursue the true culprits who were still passing bills long after Barb was arrested.

"They figured they had who they wanted, so they didn't look any further. And, it is important to note, they didn't look any further in any of the other fifty-one cases to determine who passed those particular bills. To put this in further perspective," elaborated Sanger, "long after Fraley's arrest, a number of these bills, some fifty of them, appeared in northern Idaho, eastern Washington, and even western Montana. Barb wasn't passing those; we know that for a fact. She was under strict home monitoring and was certainly not running around three different states cashing counterfeit bills. But on November 6, they actually apprehended her having passed a counterfeit hundred dollar bill at Perkins in Ritzville. That does not mean that she knew it was counterfeit."

Sanger was quick to apprise the jury of the judge's forthcoming instructions.

"You will be instructed by the court that the mere passing of a counterfeit bill does not a guilty person make."

Barb would have you note that Richard Yokum stole the purse from the bowling alley and that Harold Stegeman gifted her innocent self the phony hundreds.

Timothy Ohms, armed with impressive visual aids and a casting call of prosecution witnesses, may have outgunned Sanger in the courtroom even without arresting Barb's best defender. Harold was to take the stand and spin a believable yarn in Barb's behalf, explaining how she came into possession of several hundred dollar bills of dubious authenticity.

The story, later related to a disbelieving jury by an ill-prepared Barb, was that Harold sold a trailer for cash, the purchaser never came for the trailer, they couldn't remember his name, and the money turned out to be fake. She would have been better off sticking to the original "cashed the paycheck at the supermarket and this is what I got" story.

Tim Ohms trotted out significant participants to describe the damaging particulars. Todd Bright, manager of Perkins, took the stand with confidence and well-deserved self-assurance.

"As soon as I was given the bill, I knew it was fake. It was extremely coarse. It felt like a brown paper bag. At first I thought it was a joke; I thought, 'No, you're kidding me.' It was that obvious. It had no red threads in it, and there were blotches of ink on the borderline of the bill."

Ohms attempted to cast Barb's behavior at Perkins in the most incriminating light, implying guilt because she had "attempted to flee." Sanger condemned the inference as unwarranted and irresponsible.

"Her son, Richard, was the driver and owner of the only vehicle they had," pointed out Sanger. "Except when they were standing in front of the cash register, Richard stayed right next to Perkins Restaurant outside the front door with the manager during the entire process. The only one who didn't stick around was Harold Stegeman."

If found guilty, Barb faced the possibility of seventy-five years in jail—fifteen years maximum on each of five different counts of knowingly passing a counterfeit bill.

Her best bet—her only bet—was to make sure all the blame fell on the man who called himself Harold Stegeman. Sanger told the jury about Harold's arrest, the card from Inland Photo Supply with the flipside list of counterfeiting ingredients, Stegeman's alias of Frank Wincheski, Barb having "learned only Friday that he's not Mr. Stegeman," the government not knowing who he was or where he was from or "even if he is a citizen of the United States."

Wednesday afternoon, following Workman's testimony confirming the counterfeit nature of Stegeman's identity, Richard Sanger explained his desire to put the recently arrested Harold on the stand to Judge Van Sickle.

"Your Honor," began Sanger, "I'll be very honest with you about this because I don't want to get in any trouble, but I want the jury to see Mr. Stegeman and get some idea of what kind of person he is."

Harold and his court-appointed counsel were in another courtroom in the same building for a prerelease detention hearing. Harold could be tracked down and in the witness box within thirty minutes.

"I'm not putting him on the stand expecting him to testify at length and answer all of my questions," Sanger continued. "I fully expect to ask him questions such as 'You manufactured this money, didn't you?' and 'Who are you?' and 'You gave your wife some of this manufactured money without telling her, didn't you?' and I expect him to take the Fifth Amendment. And I am expecting him to be advised by the court in front of the jury of his Fifth Amendment rights. Now, if that is improper or if the court disapproves of it, that's fine."

It wasn't until 3:30 P.M. and out of the presence of the jury, that Van Sickle gave his opinion. In his review of the law, he determined that Mr. Stegeman may not be unavailable for inquiry by either side.

"I would give what's called the neutralizing instruction to members of the jury," explained the judge, "the court has determined that while there have been references made in this trial to Mr. Stegeman, the jury may not draw inferences from that fact or from the fact that Mr. Stegeman did not appear as a witness in the case."

Van Sickle did allow Sanger to make inquiry of Harold outside the presence of the jury. Harold R. Stegeman, the man who once elevated Shelton's Barbara Fraley to the ranks of well-kept women and pampered lovers, the former Mr. Moneybags who treated her as if she were plated in gold, was asked to take the stand.

"Please come forward here, sir. Please raise your right hand."

Whereupon, Harold R. Stegeman, having been first duly sworn at 3:35 P.M., testified.

Thirteen

You know what charm is: a way of getting the answer yes without having asked any clear question.

—Albert Camus

It was as if every atom in the universe ceased to move. The attention of every human mind and heart within the confines of the courtroom focused on the charming gentleman who swore to tell the truth, the whole truth, and nothing but the truth.

"I had no idea what he was going to say," recalled Tim Ohms. "He was going to have to say one of three things. He was going to say his name was Harold Stegeman, which was false, he was going to have to reveal his true identity, or he was just going to keep his mouth shut. I tried to be prepared for whatever it was he had to say. He only had so many options."

Barb sat transfixed. This was it. She was about to find out exactly what was going on with Harold. Since the moment of his sudden arrest at Spinardo's, she hadn't received a comprehensible answer from anyone. She had no idea why Harold was taken away;

even Harold hadn't been told why he was picked up until he was in the county jail.

"After Harold was arrested I kept calling around trying to find out what they did with him and where they took him. I finally found out that he was taken from the jail to the Federal Building because he had to waive something, whatever that means. When I got into the elevator of the courthouse, there was Lyle Workman. I immediately asked him why Harold was picked up."

Lyle erroneously, but understandably, assumed Barb knew everything about the man to whom she was married and replied, "We received Harold Stegeman's death certificate."

Barb didn't get it. Now, with her handsome husband under oath, perhaps she would understand.

The court clerk spoke: "Would you state your full name and spell your last name for the court and record."

"Your Honor, my attorney instructed me to inform the court that I would like to invoke my right under the Fifth Amendment to remain silent. With all due respect, sir."

"I understand, sir," responded the judge.

Barb did not understand at all.

Sanger began direct examination.

"Mr. Stegeman, what is your true identity?"

"I respectfully refuse to answer that question."

Harold saw the color drain from Barb's face.

"Did you manufacture counterfeit money and give some of it to your wife?"

"I refuse to answer on the same grounds."

Barb felt faint.

"Are you going to answer any of my questions, or do you refuse all questions on the same grounds?"

"I refuse to answer all questions on the same grounds."

"You may step down, sir."

Richard Sanger approached the bench; Barb approached delirium.

"I have subpoenaed Mr. Stegeman and tried to get his testimony. At this point Mr. Stegeman was not available to help the defense, maybe at some later point he would have been."

Ohms, knowing Sanger would want the judge to grant a continuance, allowing time to obtain additional evidence helpful to Barb, was not shy in voicing his objections.

"Your Honor, this defendant is charged with passing counterfeit currency. The government has not made any allegations as to who manufactured it. There's substantial evidence, not only with regard to the passing of money at Perkins, but with regard to four passes of counterfeit currency occurring on one day, from which the jury could infer guilty knowledge on the part of the defendant. I don't see how the testimony of an individual saying, 'I gave this money to someone' would be relevant for purposes of determining guilty knowledge at that point in time. I allowed Mr. Sanger to delve as deeply as he wished into any information concerning Mr. Stegeman, and I feel that he's had ample opportunity to raise any inference he wishes about Mr. Stegeman's character or his involvement in criminal conduct."

The difficulty was in determining when and if Harold Stegeman would be available to testify for the defense. It could be never. Van Sickle did not grant a continuance, and Sanger didn't expect him to. The only witness left for the defense was the defendant herself.

Sanger took a good look at his client. She did not look good. She appeared devastated and disoriented.

"My client is extremely tired at this point in time after three days in trial," pleaded Sanger, "and she did not sleep very well last night. I beg the court's indulgence in allowing us to recess for the day and begin with her testimony first thing in the morning."

The jury was brought back into the courtroom at 3:45 P.M.; court adjourned at 3:48 P.M.

On March 12, 1992, the proceedings of the final day of Barb Fraley's trial began at exactly 9:00 A.M., with defense counsel Richard Sanger making a motion to dismiss count one of the five counts against Barb—the incident at HiCo Exxon.

"There is no evidence in the State's case from which a reasonable person could find the defendant guilty beyond a reasonable doubt," insisted Sanger, taking issue with the videotaped evidence. "The government conceded in its opening statement that the jury could not make an identification from the videotape.

"They also said the tape did not show the little finger of the suspect's right hand. The suspect was either missing a finger, or the camera couldn't see it. Barb has a little finger on her right hand, only the very tip of it is missing.

"Agent Workman stated that the clothing worn by Barbara

Fraley in Ritzville is the same as the clothing seen in the HiCo incident. However, these witnesses admit that they cannot point to any distinguishing features of the clothing, that they were judging from a black and white photo, and that they could not tell the color of the clothing in the photo."

Sanger then raised an unintentionally amusing issue.

"Everybody knows that they have videotape cameras in the HiCo stores right out in plain sight for God and everybody to see. Any knowing counterfeit passer wouldn't be worthy of his trade to go in front of a camera with a counterfeit hundred dollar bill."

No one claimed Barb was worthy of the trade.

Judge Van Sickle denied Sanger's motion, and at 9:30 A.M. Barbara LeHew Yokum Fraley Stegeman took the stand on her own behalf. While she was being placed under oath, U.S. Magistrate Stephen Ayers of Coeur d'Alene, Idaho, signed a search warrant for Harold Stegeman's residence and the adjoining trailer.

"The purpose of the search," explains Lyle Workman, "was to find the passport he obtained using false identification. That's all they were looking for."

The search began at 11:50 A.M., exactly twenty minutes before court took noon recess. Special Agents Mikalson, Rosdahl, and Kircher, accompanied by Kootenai County Deputies Brodeur and Street, encountered no opposition from the home's only occupants, thirteen-year-old Leanna and sixteen-year-old Jerry.

The passport (real), Cayman Island Resident Permit #3408 (fraudulent), Social Security card #594-36-7447 (valid), and Dade County Birth Registration card #43288 (authentic) were all found in the master bedroom closet.

There was more.

From the same bedroom Special Agent Rosdahl retrieved a brown vinyl briefcase containing Barb Fraley's 1987 and 1988 tax returns. It also contained two photographic impressions of a Federal Reserve Note. One photo was a Bank Seal, the other was the lettering "This note is legal tender for all debts, public and private."

"Whose briefcase is this?" Agent Rosdahl posed the question to sixteen-year-old Jerry Fraley. Jerry said that it belonged to Harold Stegeman. In fact, he was sure of it. Rosdahl placed a call to Special Agent Neil Goodman of the Spokane field office, who obtained authorization from Magistrate Ayers for an additional search warrant to look for materials and equipment used to manufacture counterfeit Federal Reserve Notes.

"What's occurred here that is very unusual," commented Timothy Ohms several months later, "is that you have an investigation of someone who could potentially be a significant witness for the defense occurring while the defense is in a jury trial. You don't usually have a situation where the trial is Monday, and Thursday you are out searching another suspect's house, which also happens to be the defendant's house, and you find evidence. In this case, the proverbial smoking gun—the photographic impression of a Federal Reserve Bank Seal."

It was exactly 9:30 A.M. when the court clerk asked Barb to state her full name and to spell her last name for the Court and jury.

"Barbara Ellen Fraley. F-R-A-L-E-Y, is what my name was at the time. My name now is Barbara Stegeman. S-T-E-G-E-M-A-N. I believe."

Barb had no way of knowing her own last name and slim chance of overcoming the ignominious implications of the prosecution's well-executed multimedia presentation. Ohms had trotted out employees from Perkins, Señor Froggy's, and every convenience store and pie purveyor with whom Barb had supposedly come in contact. The jury was treated to videotapes, photo enlargements, and in-depth explanations of intaglio printing worthy of PBS. The twelve-person panel of her peers even heard testimony from Sharon Burgerson, the attractive nurse's aide from Holy Family Hospital who bought a twelve-pack of beer, five lottery tickets, and three bags of M&Ms at HiCo Exxon.

Barb told her story to the jury, answering questions from Ohms and Sanger. She recounted the woes visited upon her by providence, matrimony, and entrepreneur restaurateur Harold Stegeman. Barb denied any knowledge of counterfeiting in general and passing bills in specific, insisted she couldn't find the HiCo Exxon even when she went looking for it, and related the tale of Harold giving her $1,000 in one hundred dollar bills after selling a trailer.

"He says the guy gave him money down on it, but the guy never came back," explained Barb, "but the trailer is still setting there waiting. If the guy ever comes back, the trailer is his."

"Is it common," asked Ohms of Barbara, "for Mr. Stegeman to give you money in hundred dollar denominations?"

She confirmed that Harold had often given her money—plenty of money.

Did Barb, prior to Harold's arrest, have any reason to believe that her husband was involved in criminal activity?

"No," came her reply.

"Do you have some reason now to believe he was engaged in criminal activity?"

Barb wept.

"Nothing would surprise me now after finding out that he's not the person I married. He could be involved in murder as far as I know. I don't know what he's been involved in. He's not the person he said he was."

"But he always had money, didn't he?"

"Yes, that's correct."

"And you never knew where his money, the money he started with, came from, correct?"

"That's correct."

"Did you ever have any idea how much it was?"

"No, but I know he put a lot of money in the restaurant."

"Did you ever meet any of his friends?"

"No. He never had any friends. He was a loner type of person."

At 12:10 P.M., when Tim Ohms and Richard Sanger had exhausted all avenues of direct and cross-examination, the defense rested. During the lunch break, Ohms heard news from the Secret Service, which he felt compelled to share with Sanger and the court.

At 1:30 P.M. the court reconvened out of the presence of the jury. Tim Ohms was the first to speak.

"I just learned at lunch that another federal agency obtained a search warrant, I believe this morning, for Mr. Stegeman's residence, which is also this defendant's residence. It is my understanding that they obtained the warrant in order to search for Mr. Stegeman's passport. I am informed of some of the items that were discovered during the course of that search, and I disclosed the nature of those items to Mr. Sanger."

In truth, Ohms knew about the search warrant before it was served.

"Of course, I knew in advance that they were going to search Stegeman's house, which was also the defendant's house, that day. It wasn't something that came as a surprise to me, but I didn't have to tell Sanger about it until the warrant was served," elaborated Ohms. "I was kind of in a bind because it was an unusual situation. I was in no position to make any call as to what the defense could or would use on behalf of Barb Fraley. They are entitled to know anything and everything. For all I knew, Sanger wanted to use the results of the search to bolster his argument that Stegeman was the bad guy and Barb was his innocent victim. That is not for me to say, and I wanted to make sure Sanger knew exactly what was going on. I did not want to find myself in any sort of situation where the court could declare a mistrial."

Judge Van Sickle wasn't quite sure what was happening.

"All right. What do you seek to do at this time?"

"Well, I want to place that on record because some of the information or material that was discovered would ordinarily have relevance to this case. I don't intend to introduce any evidence of that nature on rebuttal, because that wasn't the intent of the search in the first place."

Ohms felt it was important to notify Sanger of the incriminating evidence found during the search and wanted it on the record. He was not about to jeopardize his case or future prosecutions by making any errors.

Van Sickle turned to Sanger.

"Anything you wish to make known to the court at this time?"

"Your Honor, as far as I know about what was discovered, it would be corroborative of the defense theory that Mr. Stegeman was the manufacturer of the bills."

However, if the new evidence also implicated Barb, he couldn't risk looking into it further.

"I don't know enough about it to ask for a continuance to explore it," said a weary Richard Sanger. "I don't know what I might run into. So, I believe that at this point in time my best option is to proceed."

The jury was supplied instructions, verdict forms, and final arguments.

The deliberations began.

"Do you think the jury doesn't read the newspaper?"

The rhetorical question comes from Richard Sanger, noting Bill Morlin's ongoing coverage of Barb and Harold's legal misadventures in *The Spokesman-Review*. On the morning after Barb's final testimony, the following headline story appeared in the local paper:

FEDERAL AGENTS FIND SIGNS
OF COUNTERFEITING

"Thursday, as Barbara Fraley told a Spokane jury she didn't know anything about counterfeit money, federal agents searched her Hayden Lake, Idaho, home and said they found evidence of a counterfeiting operation," wrote reporter Morlin. "The U.S. District Court jury wasn't told about the discovery made by Secret Service agents and a State Department investigator. The jury will resume its deliberations this morning to decide whether the forty-four-year-old mother of five is guilty of passing counterfeit money."

Richard Sanger rolled his eyes and leaned back in his creaking public defender chair. There was barely room for disappointment in his cramped, windowless office.

"I have some real problems with the way the government handled this case."

Fourteen

What we are dealing with here is a matter of perception.
—Richard Sanger
Public Defender

Lyle Workman insisted that arresting Stegeman on the verge of Barb's trial was not planned as a prosecution tactic, but was the result of last-minute confirmation that Stegeman wasn't Stegeman.

"We didn't arrest Harold to impact Sanger's defense of Barb," explained Workman. "It just happened to come at a bad time for him, and he had his hands full as it was."

Sparks flew between Sanger and Workman at the trial. Both became visibly overheated during a pointed exchange in which Sanger implied Workman withheld important information from the defense.

"This Harold Stegeman who's married to Barbara Fraley, he's been a very difficult person to check out as far as identity is concerned," began Sanger.

"Very difficult," responded Workman.

"Have you been able to find out who he really is?"

"No, sir."

Workman had already testified about the counterfeiting ingredients listed on the back of the Inland Photo Supply business card.

"Do you know what country he's a citizen of?" continued Sanger.

"No, sir."

Sanger then blindsided Workman with an unexpected question.

"When did I first learn about the card and these other businesses and this identification?"

"I'm sorry?"

Sanger rephrased the question, tingeing it with blatant bile.

"When was I first informed about the card in Stegeman's wallet and the photo supply business and the identity problem?"

"I don't know. It was in my report," Workman replied.

"A report to me?"

"It's in my memorandum report."

"Well," Sanger started to steam, "when you and I discussed this case last Wednesday or Thursday in Mr. Ohms's office, I asked you, did I not, 'What about Mr. Stegeman? Haven't you checked him out?' And you wouldn't give me any answers! Isn't that correct?"

Lyle went bolt upright in his seat.

"You know that I referred you to Mr. Ohms!"

"When?" countered Sanger. "Last Wednesday? Last Thursday? As of that time I didn't know anything about this stuff you just testified to, isn't that true?"

Sanger had cause for anger. Although Workman received Harold Stegeman's birth certificate on March 5, and Sanger was notified of that information on March 6, the day of Harold's arrest, Workman kept a separate file on Stegeman—a file containing information not shared with the defense until Stegeman was in custody.

"There was a separate file on Mr. Stegeman, and the information in Mr. Stegeman's file only relates to Mr. Stegeman," testified Workman. "It does not relate to this defendant."

The tidbits about Harold using Barb's car, Barb's son, and the alias of Frank Wincheski when purchasing counterfeiting supplies were never added to Barb's file, nor were any other aspects of Workman's investigation into possible or confirmed criminal behavior by Harold Stegeman.

"Well," Workman later explained, "they were two separate investigations. The reason for not wanting to tell [Barb] or her counsel everything I knew about Stegeman was security. It was an active investigation into Stegeman; Fraley is Stegeman's wife. It was difficult and unusual. I can see why Sanger would misunderstand and get irritated, but I couldn't jeopardize an investigation into an ongoing conspiracy."

The posttrial drive from Spokane to Hayden Lake allowed the frazzled Ms. Fraley little time for emotional decompression. The jury was deliberating, Harold, or whomever he was, was behind bars, and Barb attempted to process revelations about her counterfeit spouse amidst the chaotic intracranial residue of a grueling courtroom experience. She arrived home to find Secret Service agents, a representative of the U.S. State Department, and local law enforcement personnel crawling all over her house. No one searched the raisin box on the porch. It didn't matter. Barb had burned the last bills long ago.

Fifteen

The fishermen know that the sea is dangerous and the storm terrible, but they have never found these dangers sufficient reason for remaining ashore.

—Vincent Van Gogh

"Crime on the High Seas?" Phil laughed as if he thought it was funny. He didn't. Not that he was naive, but he was honestly hoping that Raul's desire to acquire this particular craft had nothing to do with concealed contraband.

"Contraband deluxe," confirmed the caffeinated Norwegian, "about three million dollars worth. We'll stop off the Everglades and unload it. You'll see; the boats will come and meet us." He said it as if he were talking about the weather.

Phil decided to drink rum.

"I was already in the middle of it, so what else could I do? I figured Raul had taken care of everything, so I might as well do my best to relax, wait out the voyage, and collect my money."

Phil drank and waited. Then, in the shallow waters off the Everglades, he heard the roar of cigarette boats blasting out of the swamp. Forty feet long and with high-powered engines capable of slicing saltwater at 120 miles per hour, they were smugglers' dream machines.

"These guys pulled up and we stopped. The water was glassy and calm as it usually was in the gulf," recalls Champagne. "Then they went down in the hull and started crashing around. It sounded like they were ripping open crates. I leaned against the rail lookin' at the boats rafted together along the side and ignored the whole damn thing. They started moving whatever they were yankin' out of the hull into the cigarette boats. Didn't seem like very much of whatever it was to me."

Phil Champagne put his head in his hands.

"I should have seen it comin', but what did I know?"

As Phil sipped rum and watched the transaction, the Norwegian and the leader of the cigarette crew began having an altercation. Voices got louder. It had something to do with money.

"I don't remember if anyone called out a warning. All I know is that gunfire erupted. JESUS CHRIST! Just what I needed. I dropped to my hands and knees. There was a steel rail all around the ship with scuppers under it. I remember thinking that I hoped the bullets didn't come under and hit me. I thought they were gonna murder us all sure as shit. The shooting went on, then stopped, and then I heard the roar of the boats taking off."

Phil expected to find his captain and crew in a blood-drenched pile. Nobody was even wounded.

"Yumpin' Yesus!," yelled the Norwegian, "they tried to kill us! I didn't bargain for this! Yumpin' Yesus!"

"Wait a second," barked Phil. "I don't know what you're gonna do, but let me get this straight: they took whatever that was and didn't pay for it, right?"

"Yeah."

"Christ! I'm glad my money isn't coming from there. We gotta tell Raul what happened."

They couldn't risk making a call from the ship's radio, and Phil was concerned that the gunshots had attracted the Coast Guard.

"If I were you," Phil said to the captain, "I'd turn this thing around and get out of here."

Champagne took a good look in the direction of shore.

"Hell, that's Naples over there."

Naples, Florida, was homeland to the most astonishing trackers in history—the Seminole-Negroes. Their ancestors were runaway slaves who took refuge among the Florida Seminole. The Seminole were not a nomadic or predatory people, but sedentary and civilized; hunting was subordinate to stock-raising and farming. They only took to the warpath in self-defense. So did Phil Champagne. He knew nothing of Seminoles, the early development of Naples in 1885, or when swamp buggy races became an October tradition. He only knew the best restaurants, cocktail lounges, and the phone number of one semiregular lover.

If the Norwegian and the crew were working hand in glove with the gun-toting devils who absconded with the contraband, Phil wanted off the boat and out of the game immediately.

"We got a nice sized Zodiac here," declared Phil. "I'm taking the son of a bitch and going to Naples."

And that is exactly what he did running the Zodiac full tilt until it ran right up on the beach. Finding the beach was no problem; Naples has forty-one miles of public sand. Phil threw himself at the first phone booth he saw.

"Listen, honey, I'll do anything. I'll even marry you if you want, but I got to get back to Ft. Lauderdale. Please let me borrow your car."

The odds of this particular dark-haired, thirty-five-year-old divorcee relinquishing her new silver 1985 Chevrolet Caprice Classic were remote in the extreme. She leased a new Chevy every year and babied it as some women do their poodles.

"Hell, no," said Phil's Gulfside lover, "you're not borrowing my car. I'd rather go back to my first husband than let you even get behind the wheel. Besides," she paused, "you sound like you've been sucking rum all night. If we're going anywhere, it's together. You pay for munchies and gas both ways, and I'll drive."

And she did.

"We blasted that Chevy across what we used to call Alligator Alley, the cross-state highway."

She chain smoked menthols and talked about pasta while Phil drank hot coffee and crunched his way through the greasy bag of chips they had snapped up at a convenience store.

"She always talked about pasta. If she ate all the pasta she talked about, she would've weighed 400 pounds, which, thank God, she didn't."

Phil's mind raced faster than the Chevy, computing the time lag between his departure and the ship's proposed arrival in Tampa Bay. How soon would Raul know? How fast could he get there? And, Phil wondered, what about Mike?

Phil had called Mike before the flight to Cayman, bragged about the "done deal" of two hundred grand, and proffered an invitation to a celebratory reunion.

"Give me a couple of days to make arrangements, pal," said Mike, "and don't get yourself into a jam. Remember, virtue is its own reward."

"I am, above all," insisted Champagne, "a virtuous man."

The reward Phil wanted was the $200,000. His virtue had always been generosity. The first would lead to the latter.

"When we reached Ft. Lauderdale and navigated to my moorage, I slid her gas money, a big kiss, and told her I would do something extra special for her someday. She was hoping to spend the night on the boat, but I told her that I would have to owe her one. In fact," says Phil with a grin, "I still owe her one."

Out of the car, down the ramp, onto the boat, and dead in his tracks. There was somebody already on board. A shadow moved. Quick reasoning; no problem. One man had the key. Phil hadn't expected him to arrive for another day or two, but he was happy to see him—Alias Mike.

"Man, you won't believe what happened," gasped Phil after grasping Mike's outstretched hand, "there was some sort of rip-off, and my buddy Raul doesn't even know yet."

Champagne hurriedly changed clothes, babbling details to Mike, who sat steely-eyed and intense. As an outsider, Mike soaked up the implications that washed over Phil's head.

"You know what you're going to do now?" said Mike, who was about to tell Phil what to do.

"Damn right I know," interrupted Phil, "I'm cabbing it right over to Raul's place to let him know what happened, that I had nothing to do with it, and then arrange to get my $200,000."

Mike was incredulous.

"You're nuts!"

"Nuts?"

Mike stood up and poked a stubby finger into the center of Phil's chest. Mike was smaller, but his aura was stronger.

"Forget it. Forget Raul. Forget the $200,000." Each "forget" was punctuated by a poke. "Never call. Never go there. Never go back. Get the hell out of Florida. Period."

"Mike, you're so goddamn paranoid all the time," objected Phil as he grabbed Mike's finger. "Raul is my friend. I saved his life. In fact, I bet he gives me more than $200,000 because I'm tipping him off."

Phil believed it; Mike didn't.

"Let go of my finger," said Mike.

Champagne splashed water on his face and poured himself a quick shot of vodka. There is, according to Phil, such a thing as a quick shot of vodka.

"I owe it to Raul to be straight-up with him. If I don't do this, he will be sure that I had something to do with it. You sit there, or go to the hotel. Either way, I'll be back as soon as I see Raul."

Mike pulled a .45 automatic out from under his coat as if it were a pocket watch.

"You want this, just in case?"

"Hey, this is Florida. I've got a couple of those myself. But no, I'm not taking a gun. No offense, but I don't pack heat on social calls."

Then Peter ran off to play in Mr. McGregor's garden.

Sixteen

Human beings seem to have an almost unlimited capacity to deceive themselves, and to deceive themselves into taking their own lies for the truth.

—R. D. Laing

Jerry Fraley, Leanna Fraley, Richard Fraley Jr., and the recently arrived Barbara Fraley Stegeman watched the departing entourage of law enforcement officers. The dedicated protectors of America's currency handed over an itemized list of everything seized in the search, including the incriminating negatives, identification, passport, assorted catalogues, paper stocks, and scraps of note paper. Among the scraps was a lined sheet of lavender colored paper with the following handwritten information: Gary Penar 922-2345.

"I am not an accomplice, I was not in the San Juans, and I am not a criminal," delineates Gary Penar. "I am an attorney who received a telephone call on March 6 from the magistrate's office indicating that they had an individual who was going to be testifying as a witness and they thought it would be a good idea to have him talk to an attorney before he testified. About an hour later I got a call from the same magistrate's office saying, 'He's no longer a witness; he's now been indicted. Do you still want to represent the guy?' I said, 'Sure'."

Harold, however, wasn't so sure that Penar was actually his defense attorney. His first suspicion was that Penar was a government agent pretending to be his lawyer to extract further information. After a session or two, Harold warmed up and soon intimated to Mr. Penar that he wasn't who he said he was.

"Hang on to your hat," advised Harold, "you're not going to believe this story."

Harold Stegeman then held up a yellow sheet of paper and pressed it against the glass separating the jailed defendant from his court-appointed attorney. Handwritten, for Penar's eyes only, were the astonishing details of the strange death and counterfeit resurrection of Phillip Wendell Champagne.

"When I read what he wrote, I about fell off my chair," admits Penar. "Written out in longhand was an incredible tale about falling off a boat ten years earlier, people thinking he was dead, an ex-wife and four kids, changing identities in Florida. Jesus! I just rolled my eyes."

Phil, meanwhile, was becoming increasingly afraid.

"I feared being prosecuted for not saying that I knew I was alive. Because there was insurance paid out, I knew that everybody would say 'fraud, fraud, fraud,'" laments Champagne. "That's what I was afraid of until I learned that the statute of limitations was up, and I couldn't and wouldn't be prosecuted for not being dead."

Phil also feared being charged with bank fraud.

"People were bound to figure that because I was living under another name that there had to be some intention to defraud the bank that lent me money for the restaurant. I paid back all those bank loans except the last one. The only reason the last one didn't get paid off was because I went bankrupt."

Going bankrupt under an assumed name does not, under our current justice system, meet all of the legal requirements for a legitimate bankruptcy.

"If bank fraud were the only charge against me, I would have gone to a jury trail. I never defrauded the bank, never intended to defraud the bank, and paid back every cent of every loan right up to the last. But, as I was facing counterfeiting charges, I was rather in a bind. Plus, poor, dear Barb…" Phil gets misty at the thought of Barb's courtroom distress. "She was in one room of the courthouse defending herself while I was in another room of the same courthouse to be arraigned."

Harold entered a plea of not guilty; Penar argued, to no avail, for his release.

"At that point, things were very confusing," recalls Penar. "Nobody knew who he was. They thought he was either some fellow who died in a scuba accident in the Bahamas or a British mercenary who hung out off the coast of India or a missing drug dealer/informant named Ron Kollister."

The aforementioned British mercenary, allegedly affiliated with a New York crime family and responsible for agitation in the Maldive Islands, earned his place in the mix by traveling under the alias John L. Stegeman. One Stegeman is as good as another, especially if the identification is false.

"There was a point," affirms Lyle Workman, "when I was ready to see if I could get the Secret Service to spring for me to go show Harold's picture to David Joel Friedland to see if he would say, 'Oh, yeah, I remember that guy. We used to go scuba diving together in the Cayman and Maldive Islands.' I really thought that the common ground between all these Stegemans—Friedland, the mercenary, and our Harold—was going to be drug smuggling simply because of the Miami connection."

Drug smuggling was not, according to Agent Tom Sommero, a standard component of Friedland's criminal repertoire, although Sommero acknowledged Friedland was heavily scrutinized for involvement in a variety of Florida-based insurance frauds and one rather dicey incident involving counterfeit currency.

"The samples were great; the final product was lousy," remarked Sommero, who exonerates Phil Champagne from any direct association with either Friedland or the mercenary who traveled under a Costa Rican passport.

"It is, astonishingly enough, coincidence. The Stegeman who turned up on the West Coast (Phil Champagne) had the misfortune to acquire an alias already being used by organized crime."

Neither the FBI nor Interpol ever located the elusive British mercenary, nor did they figure out the true identity of the Harold Stegeman married to Barbara Fraley. A frustrated Lyle Workman took Stegeman's fingerprints to the local Spokane Police Department. They ran a standard five-state computer check. No problem.

"Here you go, Mr. Workman. The man's name is Phillip W. Champagne."

"Criminal record?" Lyle couldn't wait to hear the juicy details.

"Well, see for yourself. Nothing for the past forty years, not even a traffic citation."

Nothing for the past forty years.

Nothing.

"I couldn't figure out why this guy Phil Champagne was so reticent about revealing his true identity," recalled Workman. "The last time he was in any trouble was way back in about 1952, and that was for taking a car without permission. What could he have to hide?"

Being dead for one thing.

Barb believed she would be found innocent. She really did.

"If the jury could only see that I was a victim. It was so obvious. I had always been a victim. How could someone who was such a good mother, such a hard worker, such a tender-hearted soul possibly be considered a criminal?"

"I had believed I would be found innocent, simply because I was innocent," recalls Mrs. Stegeman, "but the jury judged me guilty. They sent me home to await sentencing.

"On May 15, 1992, I was sentenced to ten months in Geiger Correction Center in Spokane, Washington, and two years probation. Mr. Sanger assured me that I would receive credit for the time I served on his monitor."

Sanger fought for that all the way to the Ninth Circuit Court of Appeals, but Barb never received credit for time spent on home monitor.

Seventeen

One would think that near relations, who live constantly together, and always have done so, must be pretty well acquainted with one another's characters. They are nearly in the dark about it.

—William Hazlitt

Barb, *sans* Harold, sat home with Jerry and Leanna; Harold sat in the Spokane County Jail. At the March 30 hearing, Timothy Ohms appeared on behalf of the United States while Gary Penar again represented Harold Richard Stegeman. As the defendant and his counsel were walking in to the courtroom, Tim Ohms pulled Penar aside.

"Well, we think we know for sure who he is."

Big deal. Penar already knew.

"I argued that Mr. Stegeman had opportunity and incentive to flee after the November arrest, but did not flee. In addition," Penar notes "Harold had ties to the community and opportunity for employment at Hayden Lake. Therefore, I reasoned, Mr. Stegeman need not be detained."

Timothy Ohms contended that Harold's true identity was still not known.

"Although an alias of Ronald Kollister has been investigated as [his] true identity, there is additional evidence that his true identity may be Phillip Wendell Champagne. The confusion surrounding Mr. Stegeman's true identity invalidates any of the background information that defense counsel raises to support the motion for defendant's release."

The judge sided with Ohms; Harold Stegeman stayed in jail.

Since the authorities were onto Phil's real name, he told Penar that it might be a good idea to make contact with Mitch before the shocking revelations hit the headlines.

It was a fairly one-sided conversation.

"Hello, is this Mitch Champagne? Mr. Champagne, my name is Gary Penar. I am an attorney in Spokane, Washington, and what I am about to say, you may find hard to believe...I am calling to tell you that your brother, Phil Champagne, is not dead...No, this isn't some kind of joke...Your brother, Phil Champagne, is alive and he is currently in custody in the Spokane County Jail facing charges of counterfeiting...Hello?...Mr. Champagne?"

"I wasn't asking for a response from Mr. Champagne; I just wanted to let him know that his brother was alive. That's what Phil asked me to do, so I certainly did it. Phil wanted his kids and Mitch to know that he was alive. I think Mitch was stunned, and I don't know if he believed me or not."

Disbelieving or not, Mitch was soon faced with more than enough evidence of his brother's resurrection. Within days the headlines were everywhere.

DEATH FAKER FAKED FUNDS

FAKE MONEY SUSPECT MAY HAVE FAKED DEATH

"Alleged insurance fraud is the reason Phillip Wendell Champagne was living in North Idaho, under the name Harold Richard Stegeman, according to U.S. Secret Service agents."

As reported by Bill Morlin, the story in the *Spokesman-Review* asserted that Phil faked falling off a yacht in Puget Sound to collect a $1.5 million life insurance policy.

Barb Fraley, still unsure of her legal last name, read about the past life of Phil Champagne in the morning newspaper. First fake bills, then a fake husband, now the revelations of Harold's real life family history—brothers, children, an ex-wife, an elderly mother still very much alive—and an insurance company mad as hell.

"You son of a bitch," barked Barb when Harold called collect from jail, "why didn't you tell me?"

Simple. She had never asked.

"Barb never asked me anything about my past. I told her not to because I couldn't and didn't want to lie. I promised that someday I would tell her everything."

Welcome to someday.

"Back when we were living in Shelton, we would occasionally drive through Portland to visit Barb's son in Salem. I always wore a hat and sunglasses to avoid being recognized," admits Phil. "Although this action was odd, Barb, never acted as if she noticed."

She noticed.

Phil would also sneak off for clandestine meetings from time to time with Alias Mike. Again, Barb never asked questions.

"That made me love her all the more," says Champagne with a smile. "She is always so accepting, so trusting, so willing to overlook my faults or unusual behavior."

Facing seventy-five years in prison and a maximum fine of $1.2 million because one's husband dabbled in the art of absurd counterfeiting would tend to stretch even the most accepting woman's forgiving nature, especially if her husband was revealed to be a different person entirely.

Barb, bless her heart, did more than accept and forgive.

"Of course, I still love you," said Barb to her incarcerated spouse. "I don't care if you're Harold or Phil. I married a man, not a name."

"I am the luckiest man in the world," declared Phil, weeping his way back to his cell.

"If he had told me from the beginning, I don't know if I would have stayed with him or not," says Barb. "I thought I knew him, and then, all of a sudden, I didn't know if I did or not. The only thing I ever knew about him was that he was born in Seattle and that his dad had drowned in Blue Lake."

Barb had a hard time comprehending her husband's concern, or lack of it, toward his original family.

"How did he face Christmas and all those things without ever contacting his mother or his kids? Of course, I was raised different. I came from a real close family."

But Barb wasn't the one presumed dead, and Barb's family had adopted Harold as their own.

"He may be Phil Champagne, gentleman crook to the Secret Service," stated Monte LeHew, owner of the infamous doghouse hideaway of Stegeman's bogus bills, "but he will always be good ol' Harold to me. He was always wonderful to Barb's kids and treated her like she was gold-plated. He was, and is, a real nice guy."

Phil's original family was admittedly stunned to discover that not only was he alive, but behind bars.

"I kept telling Phil that he had better call and talk to his kids," said Barb, "but he was afraid of what they might say to him. His daughter Renee called me when I was in Hayden Lake on the home monitor awaiting sentencing. She called me and said, 'I don't know how to say this, but I'm Phil's daughter.'"

Phil screwed up his courage and called Kathy and Renee at Kathy's house in Portland. Kathy wouldn't talk, but Renee was eager to hear her father's voice.

"I don't remember what was said word for word, except that I would try to explain sometime why I did what I did. Renee said 'I don't care about explanations. I understand. I'm just glad that you're alive.'"

Barb had to put all of her household goods in storage, find a secure home for her two minor children, and emotionally prepare herself for imprisonment.

"I had not had any luck finding anyone to take my youngest girl, and then Renee came to the rescue. She and her husband offered to take care of Leanna for the full ten months of my sentence. They were wonderful to all of us, supportive in so many ways."

Phil Champagne doesn't stint on his expressions of appreciation either.

"Anytime we needed anything, we could depend on Renee and her husband, Steve. They certainly have my praise and appreciation. They stood by me, Barb, and did everything they could to help."

Despite Phil penning a written apology entreating their patience and understanding, the remaining Champagne children remained immeasurably aloof.

"I really didn't want the kids to come see me in jail. It would be too humiliating. I was embarrassed enough, shamed enough, as it was. I don't think Mitch was too eager to see me, not with Federal Kemper hounding him to return the money they had paid out. For a long time I couldn't bring myself to even think about poor John Robin having been blamed all these years for my death, now knowing that I was alive."

John Robin heard of Phil's resurrection from Ed Grass, who saw it in the newspaper.

"I said, 'Get me a copy of that paper,' then I called Mitch and he said that he had heard from Phil and it was true. At first I thought it had to be a mistake. I couldn't see any way that he could have survived. I retraced my steps a thousand times to see where I went wrong, what I could have done to save him. Maybe he swam in the wrong direction, perhaps he swam toward lights that were farther away. I don't know. But when I first heard that he was alive, I thought it couldn't be true."

Eighteen

The fear of death is the most unjustified of all fears, for there's no risk of accident to someone who's dead.
—Albert Einstein

"Hey man, I'm lucky to be alive," said Phil.

"Not for long, you stupid gringo," growled Raul.

It was not the welcome Phil had anticipated. Banging on Raul's door, he was initially greeted with friendly surprise from his good buddy and two Hispanic gentlemen Phil had met at the party.

"How did you get here so soon? Come in and tell me what happened."

Phil asked if anyone had contacted Raul about anything. The answer was negative in the extreme.

"When I told him about the guys taking the goods, shooting their guns, and all that, he changed. He became totally different, and all three of them started talking in Spanish. They were very excited."

Raul invited Phil into the kitchen for a drink and conversation.

"The reason I want you to come in the kitchen," explained Raul as Phil looked for evidence of refreshment or hospitality, "is so you won't bleed all over my carpet."

Bleed?

There was a gun at Phil's head. Not a big gun, but a gun nonetheless.

"Sit in that chair and stay there, you dumb gringo, or I'll blow your fucking head off."

Phil sat down. If there was ever a time for Champagne to pour on the charm, this had to be it. Charm, however, is difficult when you are losing control of your bladder.

"What's wrong?" entreated Phil. "Do you think I took your goods?"

"Shut up! You're so dumb you couldn't steal anything from me! You're supposed to be dead!"

Raul didn't know the half of it. Phil, perceptive in the face of certain death, chose pleading as a viable option.

"I thought you were my friend. You said we were brothers. You said that was the Cuban way," simpered Phil, his knees knocking together like boney castanets.

"Cuban? Did I say I was Cuban? You're so stupid! I'm not Cuban. They're not Cuban. For all you know we could be from Mexico, Honduras, Peru, Columbia, Panama, or from the goddamn state of Texas! It's a good thing you're in the kitchen," reaffirmed Raul. "I can clean the blood off the tile."

It was beginning to look as if Raul's "good friend, Peter Donovan" was not going to get the $200,000.

"For Christ's sake," pleaded Phil, "what have I ever done to you?"

"For one thing," Raul replied, "you fucked my sister."

Perhaps Raul needed personal boundary clarification, but Phil sensed it was not the time to recommend professional counseling.

"I knew my number was up for sure. Raul was ranting and raving about how all of us on the boat were supposed to be dead. Apparently the guys in the cigarette boats were supposed to kill us all, take the stuff, and leave the boat adrift. Don't ask me why. They didn't kill anybody, so Raul was doubly pissed. He said at least he would have the pleasure of killing me himself. I was so scared, I almost fainted. I forced myself to think about my situation. The only chance I could see was the large window to my right. I figured I might be able to throw myself against it with enough force to go through. I would probably get cut to ribbons, but I might survive."

One of the three was on the telephone. From what Phil understood with his limited grasp of Spanish, they needed to either know something or get permission before they could shoot him.

"I wasn't clear on the exact nature of the conversation, except that it was highly animated and involved me. Maybe they were discussing a good place to dump the body. I was in shock and everyone seemed to move in slow motion. I sat like a pasty-faced statue, not hardly moving a muscle, watching as one of Raul's henchmen pointed the gun around the room. I imagine that had it been a movie, I would have jumped up and kicked the shit out of all of'em because they weren't holding the gun on me like I was someone they were really afraid of."

Phil turned slightly to get his feet under himself so he could take a life or death lunge at the glass. He didn't take the lunge; he took a look. Through the window, beyond the glare and darkness, was Alias Mike.

"The one guy was off the phone, but the three men were still talking in Spanish and very involved in what they were saying. Knowing I was helpless, they paid almost no attention to me as long as I just sat in the chair. I could see Mike making a questioning motion, so when they weren't looking, I ran my finger quickly across my throat in a gesture that anyone would understand. In an instant, Mike was gone."

Ding-dong. Back door bell.

The air was ice.

Raul put his finger to his lips and lowered the gun to his side. They all looked at the door. Raul faked a cheery voice.

"*Un momento, por favor.*"

Raul cautiously turned the door knob and opened the door a crack to see who was there.

WHAM!

The door burst open with such swift and sudden violence, it was as if the room warped into a grainy late show reality—Standing rock solid in the kicked-open doorway leveling an automatic with deadly accuracy was Alias Mike.

In fiction, they call it a dramatic pause. In fact, it was an instant. Six deafening rounds of chaos and cordite roared in the tiled kitchen; three bodies jerked, shuddered, and thudded to the floor.

"Raul was the first to be hit. The next two got it in rapid succession. They were all hit a second time by the three shots that immediately followed. It was deafening—BOOM! BOOM! BOOM! BOOM! BOOM! BOOM! They were all dead before they fell."

Phil and Mike got the hell out as fast as they could, walking rapidly toward the main highway and the busier area. If anyone had heard the shots, their reaction was not immediate. No one paid any attention to the two gentlemen out for a stroll.

"We made it to a store with an outside phone and called a cab and made it back to the boat. Mike took a rat tail file and ran it down the barrel of the gun. He filed the hell out of the firing pin and washed his hands with chlorine bleach. Then he disassembled the gun and threw it in one of the canals."

Back at the boat, Mike decided to call another cab, return to his hotel, and fly back to the Northwest with his pilot ex-relative. Before leaving, he gave Phil one last piece of advice.

"I strongly suggest you get the hell out of town, and do it now," Mike said as he packed a few remaining items. "Call me in a few days and let me know that you're still alive."

Alone on the boat, Phil poured himself a drink. His legs were still shaking. Three dead. Crime on the high seas. Two hundred thousand dollars sitting in a banker's box at Raul's ranch.

And then Phillip Wendell Champagne had a flash of either insanity or inspiration. The audacity of the idea and the giddy improbability were incapable of withstanding logical scrutiny, but Phil had abandoned logical scrutiny the night he fell off John Robin's boat.

Phil banged the glass on the table, went to a drawer, and took out a gun. There was $200,000 in a dead man's safe somewhere over the Georgia border with Peter Donovan's name on it. This was it, the moment of truth. There was only one way he could pull it off, but he was determined to give it a try. Phil loaded the gun and scrambled through his address book for a phone number.

"Hey, listen, this is Peter Donovan...yeah, fine...Listen, I've got an emergency. I need your help and I need it now. You're the only guy I can turn to, the only one who can help me. Yeah. You bet. I'm on my way."

Champagne pocketed the gun, grabbed his checkbook, and hailed a cab.

"Damn!" said Phil to himself, "that money is mine and I'm gonna get it!"

Nineteen

It takes a sharp observer to tell innocence from assurance.
—Charles Dudley Warner

The ammo loaded by the United States government for use against Phil Champagne was, for both Gary Penar and his client, too powerful to ignore.

"After Barb was found guilty and her sentencing came down, Phil knew he was in for a rough time," notes Penar.

"They had him pretty clean on the counterfeiting charge. I think Phil decided to cooperate early on. He was sort of glad that the ruse was over."

Lyle Workman and Timothy Ohms had no interest in locking up Phil Champagne and throwing away the key. Quite the contrary. As do most people, Lyle and Tim took a liking to the former Mr. Stegeman.

"The approach we were coming from was not that we wanted Phil to do hard time, we just wanted to make sure we got all the money and all the plates. We wanted to get to the bottom of this thing."

Champagne and Penar decided to cut a deal. Phil would plead guilty to anything and everything they wanted to toss at him, and he would take the role as mastermind of a criminal organization, tell them absolutely everything in detail, and make sure they recovered every possible bill, plate, or trace of his counterfeiting operation. The government, in return, would recommend to the court that Phil receive the minimum sentence and agree not to pursue any further charges against Barb, Monte LeHew, Richard Fraley Jr., Danny LeHew, or Monte's dog. In short, if Phil told everything, olly olly oxen free.

"We promised to cooperate fully with the government," confirms Penar, "and we did; we showed them where things were buried in the woods. As part of the agreement, they brought a polygraph in operated by a guy out from San Francisco. They set it up at the Spokane County Jail, hooked Phil up to it, then asked him all sorts of questions to make sure he was telling the truth. I got tired of hanging around, and they kind of asked me to leave anyway, so I told Phil that if there was any problem or any question he didn't feel comfortable with, to give me a call."

Two hours later, Phil called.

"Gary, I got a problem here."

"What's that, Phil?"

"Did I ever tell you about the twenties?"

"Twenties?" Gary paused. "No, Phil, you never told me anything about twenties."

"Oh. Well, I guess you should know that I also made a stack of twenty dollar bills. I never passed any. No one ever passed any, but I made them."

Once again they traipsed out to the woods and dug up the remnants of the twenty dollar plates.

Phil laughed when he heard the story recounted.

"Yeah, I made twenty dollar bills, but they looked pretty bad and felt worse. The only way you could ever pass one would be to hand it to a blind drunk who had a bag over his head and was wearing heavy gloves. I tried all manner of denominations as test runs. I just forgot to tell Gary about those."

Penar regards Champagne as one of his more delightfully entertaining clients.

"The one thing about Phil that bothers me is this: if he had put the same effort into a legitimate enterprise, he would have made a lot more money. My impression of Phil is that he got in over his head, had an unpleasant situation he could no longer deal with, and took off to have a new life. Had he resisted the temptation to counterfeit, he probably could have gone on the rest of his life without ever being 'caught.' He could have lived out the rest of his days as Harold Stegeman. But he made a decision to go for what looked like easy money. But it wasn't easy, and it wasn't real."

The Maltese Falcon also wasn't real, but unlike Sam Spade, Phil Champagne was willing to take the fall and play the sap. Barb still insists she is innocent. Phil still insists she isn't. Interestingly, this is not a source of conflict between them. Her denial and his affirmation serve the same purpose—protecting Barb. Although she was found guilty of passing bad bills, Phil may have feared additional charges would be made against her once the extent of the counterfeiting operation was known.

"Phil promised to tell us the truth," affirms Lyle Workman, "and he told us that Barb was in on it almost from the get-go. I believe him 100 per cent. But hypothetically speaking—and I do mean strictly hypothetically—if Barb was innocent and Phil feared that we would prosecute her for conspiracy to manufacture, if he didn't say she was guilty, it might make sense to him to implicate her in order to protect her. The truth of the matter is that we would not have gone after her anymore than we already did, but if in his mind he imagined that the only way for her to be protected from future charges was for him to say she was guilty, he would certainly take that position. After all, it was because of Phil's cooperation that we never went after Monte LeHew or Richard Fraley Jr. So, by saying Barb was in on it, she would be safe."

Farfetched? Certainly. Neither Lyle Workman nor Tim Ohms buys it for a minute, but few aspects of Phil's story have been anywhere within the bounds of basic rationality. Such was the case when Phil found himself flying several thousand feet above Georgia.

Twenty

It is by surprises that experience teaches all she deigns to teach us.

—Charles Sanders Pierce

"I know right where we're going; just follow the river," advised Phil.

"Gotcha, pal," said Stretch. "I just wish we had a helicopter so we could set down. I don't know what you're into, Pete, but I'd be right there with ya, both guns blazin'."

There are people in this world who will jump at adventure without a second thought. In fact, the very act of jumping is their first thought. When Phil took his first static line jump with some friends from Ft. Lauderdale, Stretch was piloting the plane. It was Stretch who became his occasional drinking buddy, Stretch who was always a wink and a nod away from illegality. Stretch had a plane, accepted checks from people he knew, and didn't ask questions. Phil wrote Stretch a perfectly good check for $2,600 to put him in a parachute, fly him over Raul's ranch, and toss him out of the plane.

"I'm sorry to get you up at this time of the morning, Stretch, but it's urgent," explained Phil when he showed up at Stretch's trailer at an ungodly hour of the morning. "I know that if I were a woman, you wouldn't mind."

"Hey, it's okay. It's okay," Stretch assured him. "What's happening? What do ya need?"

"Listen, I'm in a lot of trouble. I've got to go up over the border into Georgia, and I gotta get there before anybody else does. I'm willing to pay. I think the only way I can get into where I'm going is to jump. I know you're into this shit, so I bet you can get me a parachute, and we can pull this off."

Stretch lit up like Gabby Hayes in an old B Western.

"If you need some help, I got a couple buddies who have automatic weapons. We can go get them."

"No, I've got a gun, but I don't think I'll need it. All I gotta do is get there, grab something, and get the hell out."

Stretch started pulling things together.

"I can get everything you need in fifteen minutes," insisted Stretch when Phil told him that he would pay $2,600. "I'll take the money, but I'd do it just for the fun of it. This is my kind of job. But you won't have to jump if I can set down. Honest, I can land my plane on a dime. Then I can fly you out."

Phil wished it could be that way, but he knew that without a helicopter there was no way to land.

"I think the plane was a Cessna 185," says Champagne, doing his best to remember details, "but where the doors open on the right-hand side, most airplanes have a little door you open so you can climb in the back or the front. Well, this had been cut out and it had a door that folded up to the wing and fastened and dropped down. Stretch said it was for skydiving and 'dropping other things.' The way it worked was simple: you step out on the side, put a foot on that thing, and then the step went out to the wing. You just grab hold of the hand-holds and go when you're gonna go."

For one brief moment prior to take off, Phil almost came to his senses and gave it up. The moment passed, and at 7:45 A.M. the two men took off into the Florida skies.

"Stretch was familiar with the area, and when I described the terrain I saw the first time I flew up with Raul, he knew what I was talking about. We flew, refueled once, and then kept on going. I could easily find the place, it was no trouble at all. Different things went through my mind, like 'What if I can't find it?' So what? We found it easy enough."

There was the river. It all looked familiar.

"Follow that turn, keep going, look for the next turn in the river...," Phil directed.

Phil figured chances were good that no one could have moved fast enough to beat him to the ranch.

"We flew over the house at thirty-five hundred feet, checking it out for cars or helicopters which would tell me if anyone was there."

No helicopter, no car, not even the caretaker's pickup.

Phil mused out loud as they circled overhead, "Not a soul is home, not even servants. I don't think anyone is there at all."

"I see a good place to set down," Stretch interrupted, "but it would be a lot easier if we had a chopper. If there's anyone to see you, they might see you when you jump."

"Jesus, Stretch, I didn't exactly have a lot of time to plan this. I'm just gonna jump and take my chances."

Stretch circled several miles from the house, bringing the plane to exactly twenty-five hundred feet.

"I'll tell you when to go. If I could I would go with you, you know I would."

Phil opened the door.

"I never once thought of changing my mind and going back. At that moment, I knew I was a different person than I had been a few years earlier."

Stretch wished Pete all the luck in the world. Knowing he'd need it, Phil accepted the wish.

Champagne jumped, and the earth rushed up to meet him.

"I never saw Stretch again, but I made sure his check cleared the bank before I closed out the account," said Phil. "I wanted to make sure he got paid in full."

When Phil finally came back to earth, he landed in a field of tall grass a quarter mile from the house. He folded the chute, took off his jump gear, hid the stuff in nearby bushes, and waited to see if anyone had noticed him.

"I made my way through the pasture, open land, deep grass, hedgerows, and those pine woods. As I crept toward the house, the dogs came rushing at me, barking like crazy until they realized that they knew me. I calmed them down because I knew that if there was someone in the house all that dog noise would bring 'em out."

Phil heard a door open. He crouched in the bushes and waited. Sure enough, someone was in the house and had stepped out to the patio to see why the dogs were barking.

"I'll be damned," Phil said to himself. "I know that guy."

Phil was pissed.

He had risked life and limb for the box of loot only to find there was an unexpected house guest at Raul's country estate. The mystery guest wasn't one of Raul's regular buddies, nor was he someone Phil Champagne had seen in Florida before. He was a familiar face from days gone by.

"I moved around the house and peered in the windows," details Champagne. "I couldn't see anyone else inside. When I heard him return to the house, I carefully moved back toward the patio, slid up alongside the patio door, and looked in. He was watching television with his back to me."

Phil decided to take the direct approach and rely on the element of surprise. He pulled out his .45 and took a deep breath.

"I walked through those French doors like I was Alan Ladd; that son of a bitch almost soiled his shorts when he saw me standing there with my automatic aimed at his heart. I hoped he couldn't tell how bad my hands were shaking."

The startled occupant froze in fear, his eyes fixed in stark terror. What he was seeing was impossible but true Peter Donovan had come back from the dead.

Again.

"Stick 'em up," growled Phil. "Reach for the sky."

Twenty-One

But the kind of deceit that is treachery is quite another matter.

—*Julian Jaynes*
The Origin of Consciousness in the Breakdown of the Bicameral Mind

The man in Phil's sights made a feeble attempt to stand and an equally inept foray into the world of babbling explanations.

"Sit down and shut up!" ordered Phil. "What do you know about Raul?"

"He's...he's dead...and two others," stammered the trembling captive. "They found the bodies...no one knows who...why...no cops...can't afford..."

Phil cut him off with a glare and a gesture.

"You know who blew them away? Me! I did it," lied tough guy Champagne. Having the upper hand, Phil felt entitled to play the badass. "Now how about you? You wanna try something? Feel lucky? Well, do ya, punk?" Phil said with bravado.

"I was probably as scared as he was," remembers Champagne, "but I had a gun; he didn't. Plus I was mad as hell. After all, this jerk was the same one who stood on the dock at Cancun and motioned to the guys with the high-powered rifles to blow Sam and me away. The son of a bitch had tried to kill me, for God's sake."

Any machismo left in the icy veins of the fearful fellow cowering in the chair evaporated in the heat of the moment. It was the bad guy's turn to plead for mercy.

"I'll tell you whatever you want to know, honest. I was only following orders," whimpered Miguel.

"Go on," prompted Phil, "let's hear it."

"When you first came to Merida, I called Raul and asked him what to do. You knew all the passwords, but I didn't trust you; there was something funny about you. I thought you were a Fed or some kind of special agent. We already figured that Sam was a snitch. Raul told me to make you think you were in, then get rid of you."

"Ya missed, stupid, and," Phil added with disdain, "you shot up a perfectly good boat." Phil liked rubbing it in.

"Then," continued Miguel, "a long time later, I saw you at a nightclub here in Florida. First I was afraid you'd seen me. After a while, I knew you hadn't. I called Raul, and he came to the club to take a look."

"And?"

"Can I put my hands down?" asked Miguel hopefully.

"No, you can shove them up your ass or put them on the top of your head, whichever is more comfortable."

Miguel put his hands atop his head and continued.

"When Raul arrived, you were doing your German act for your friends. He told me to stay out of sight and said, 'We can use this dummy to cure our problem in the Cayman Islands.'"

Dummy?

"Yumpin' Yesus," intoned Phil, shifting his weight and releveling his .45. "You mean the whole damn thing about the scuba diving accident and saving his life was a setup? What a bunch of dirty, stinking bastards."

Phil sat down wearily behind Raul's desk, resting his right elbow from the weight of the gun, and stared at the nattily dressed but profusely perspiring criminal. The man looked empty, shrunken, and impotent. The only sound in the room came from the television. An attorney was advertising his services for victims of personal injury or wrongful death.

"They thought I was some sort of goddamn Lyle Workman," recounts Phil with a bemused laugh. "I guess they could tell there was something unusual about me, that I had something to hide, but all I was hiding was that I was supposed to be dead. Once this jerk laid it all out for me, it seemed pretty damn transparent. After all, when I was in Cancun he told me that he wanted me to deliver that sailboat to Marathon. I had put that whole awful episode out of my mind, so I never even thought of there being any connection between my nightmare in Mexico and my good buddy Raul, may he rot in Hell."

Phil popped open the panel and took out the box. It was all still there—the money and the note. Peter Donovan read it aloud.

"See?" said Phil when we was done reading, "I'm just here to claim what's mine."

"What about me?" Miguel was desperate.

"You don't get any," joked Phil. "You don't deserve a cent."

That was not what Miguel had meant.

"You're going to kill me," he said, as if announcing a ball score. "Fuck you, then. Get it over with."

Phil Champagne had no intention of killing anyone.

"For God's sake, all you lowlifes know how to do is rip each other off and shoot people. I swear, you give criminals a bad name. All I'm gonna do is tie you up and walk away. I let you live; you never say a word. That's the deal. You never saw me; I never saw you."

Maybe Miguel saw the last meaningless minutes of his life washing away on the red mist rolling over his eyes. He had told men that they were not going to die knowing full well that they would soon be bloody, lifeless, and stuffed in the trunk of a car or weighted to the bottom of the ocean. Perhaps his internal mental projector played back every incident of mayhem and carnage which he had dispassionately directed. Perhaps not.

For whatever reasons, fueled by whatever emotions, Miguel failed to believe the honest promise of the man known to him as Peter Donovan. Miguel decided that if he was going to die, he would go down fighting. All he needed was an opportunity. He knew exactly which drawer of Raul's desk contained a loaded .38 revolver.

Phil stood up with the banker's box under his left arm and

moved away from the desk. He was looking for something to restrain the increasingly distraught Miguel. He walked across the room and turned off the television, terminating the irritating sales pitch for audio cassettes on how to get rich in real estate.

With the television off, Phil heard the distinctive rumble of the caretaker's pickup coming down the road.

Champagne glanced from Miguel to the window and back. Miguel was out of the chair.

"Stop!" yelled Phil. "Stop, goddamn it!"

Miguel lunged over the desktop, threw open the top right drawer, and spun around clutching a .38 revolver.

"Don't!"

He did.

"I'll be damned if the son of a bitch didn't try to kill me again," says Champagne. "I could have shot him anytime, but I wouldn't. And there he is in a hot sweat panic lying sideways across Raul's desk pointing that .38 right at me. The little prick even pulled the trigger. Scared the hell out of me."

The shot went wild, but for all Phil knew, Miguel had shot him. All he heard was gunfire, round after round. All except the first came from the .45.

"I felt my gun going off in my hand. Once, twice, then again. I was firing out of fear and reflex; I wasn't aiming."

Bullets slammed into the wood desk right by Miguel, splinters flew everywhere, and he went flailing off to the right. The crack when his head hit the table was almost as loud as the gunfire.

His gun did a loop-de-loop and plopped on the carpet.

Miguel's limp body lay against the wall on the opposite side of the desk by the coffee table, but Phil saw no bloodstains.

"The dumbshit either knocked himself out cold by hitting his head on that coffee table, or he fainted out of sheer fright. Maybe the little prick had a well-deserved heart attack. I don't know and I don't really care. I would have been perfectly happy to have shot him, but I don't have Mike's aim or Mike's nerve."

Phil was not about to give CPR or call 911; he headed for the breezeway. His ride had arrived.

"They had just stopped the truck by the carport and the two of them had stepped out when I showed up brandishing that .45. I said, 'Go on, move, I'm borrowing the truck,' and I used my most gruff and commanding voice."

One of the caretakers turned and ran toward the back of the house, the other followed, so Phil took time to unload the groceries before driving away.

"Yes, I unloaded their groceries," says Champagne with a hearty laugh. "I guess I figured they needed them. I don't know. You do strange things when you've just been in a gunfight."

Phil and his $200,000 cruised twenty miles from where Raul's road turned off from the secondary highway. He ditched the pickup and caught a bus to a larger city where he caught another bus to Miami. The .45 eventually wound up in the bottom of a swamp, and Phil, still clutching the box, rode a taxi back to his boat in Ft. Lauderdale.

"I thought, 'What the hell.' I knew it could be dangerous, but I had gone so far already, I grabbed what belongings I needed and checked into a motel. The next day I called a boat broker with a story about how I had to move it fast, preferably for cash, and I was willing to sell it at a greatly reduced price."

In the best of scenarios, the broker would have found a wealthy character in Ft. Lauderdale eager to fork over hard cash for huge savings. Phil's life was seldom the best of scenarios. The broker found an eager buyer in Tampa. Phil would have to deliver the boat and take a check.

Checking accounts had been driving Phil crazy ever since he returned from Georgia. When a man has over $200,000 in cash—there was more than the promised amount in the box—he has to put it somewhere.

"I opened so many checking accounts at so many different branches under so many different names, it was hard to keep track," remembers the man of a thousand monikers. "I would deposit a few thousand more in cash every day, then write myself checks to move the money around. I always made sure they were noninterest bearing accounts so there were no problems."

What Phil Champagne needed was a new identity, not just another phony name. He needed a birth certificate, driver's license, social security number, and a U.S. Passport. He needed to become someone solid.

Harold Richard Stegeman was the perfect someone.

"I had been checking into this new identity business, because I knew that once I had an established identity, I could put all the money into interest bearing accounts or CDs, pay my taxes like a good American, and go somewhere and lead a normal life. I picked out Harold Stegeman as my new identity after visiting several graveyards. Hell, with the boat sold, I had enough to retire."

Phil represented himself as acting on behalf of relatives interested in documenting the Stegeman family history and paid the required fee for little Harold's birth certificate. The birth certificate enabled Phil to acquire a social security number. He then manufactured a Cayman Islands Driver's License and Resident Permit which, in conjunction with the birth certificate, allowed him to obtain a real Florida license.

"I took the driver's test and they never asked me for any other identification, even though I had it on me just in case."

Armed with all manner of authentic and fraudulent identification, securing the U.S. passport was no problem. It wasn't legal, but it worked.

"I opened a checking account at the Pinellas Park branch of NCNB, took the boat to Tampa, and got paid $105,000. The buyer paid the broker, and the broker, after deducting his commission, wrote a check to the corporation that owned the boat."

As the finances were becoming complicated, Phil turned to the Tampa attorney who set up his ownership of the boat in the first place, the same attorney who represented his ex-flame, Ann.

"I simply endorsed that check over to the attorney. He then issued two checks. Let's say one was to Don Carlson and one was to Joe Cook. As I was them," explains Phil with adolescent laughter, "I endorsed them over to Harold Richard Stegeman and made a deposit. Then I started writing myself checks out of my other accounts, too. As I had a real social security number, I was able to invest that money in CDs and earn interest. It didn't take long before all my money was in the name of Harold Stegeman."

Armed with an NCNB Checkmate Visa debit card, Harold Stegeman had immediate ATM access to over $300,000, petty cash in his pocket, and a bright future ahead of him. He bought a new travel trailer and pointed it west.

"I've got it made," thought Harold. "I've got a real name and plenty of money. Now all I need is a nice quiet town with nice quiet people. Hell, if I pick the right spot, build a house, maybe open a little business, no one will hardly even know I'm there."

Of all the places on Earth, Harold picked Shelton.

"I can't give you a good reason why I picked Shelton," admitted Champagne, "except that maybe in the back of my mind I was hoping to be seen, to somehow have it be known that I was alive."

As true as the maxim, "Wherever you go, there you are," is the corollary, "Wherever you are is where you were going."

Phil went to prison.

The phrase "bank fraud" does not have a nice ring to it. No need to ask for whom the bell tolls, the Feds were ringing up new charges against Phil Champagne.

Phil pleaded guilty to swearing falsely in a bankruptcy court action in 1989 and lying on his application for a bank loan in 1988. The lie was being Harold Stegeman when he borrowed $5,000 from Puget Sound Bank in Shelton, then listed that loan as a debt in his bankruptcy filing the next year. A Seattle judge imposed an additional six months to Champagne's sentence.

"Under my deal with the government, I pleaded guilty to everything," acknowledges Champagne. "I also pleaded guilty to a federal charge filed in Florida accusing me of making false statements in an application for a U.S. passport."

Prosecuting Attorney Rolf Tangvald offered his observations and recommendations concerning appropriate punishment in the passport case.

"Sentencing in this can involve anything from zero to five years in prison, one to five years probation, and up to a $2,000 fine. The government is recommending that the low end of the sentence be imposed. The reason is that we would like to assist Mr. Champagne in getting his criminal past cleaned up. It was not the intention of either the government or of the defense counsel to impose additional sentence upon him."

The court agreed, added no further jail time to Phil's sentence, but charged a $100 special assessment. Wisely, Phil did not pay it with money from under Monte LeHew's doghouse.

It could have been worse. Prosecutor Rolf Tangvold contacted Seattle Postal Inspector Mike Parry requesting help to develop a viable conspiracy and mail fraud case from the 1982 accident and Federal Kemper's subsequent payment to Mitch Champagne. In May 1992, as part of the investigation, Inspector Parry and Sheriff's detective Brent Cornwall traveled to Boise, Idaho, for a little chat with Larry Wills.

"It was like he had seen a ghost," recalls Parry. Wills had read of Phil's survival and was not particularly thrilled about the implications. If Phil's fall from the *Warlock* was no accident, if the whole thing was a scam, Wills could be the most important and least questioned player in the game. Wills steadfastly clung to his original statements. If the Champagne brothers had faked Phil's death, Larry Wills believed he had also been deceived "to add credibility" to the night's events. Wills cut short his interview with Parry and Cornwall, reiterating his complete innocence of any complicity in suspected wrongdoing.

Undaunted, Postal Inspector Parry continued the mundane task of developing a mail fraud case while the prosecuting attorneys pondered a puzzling legal conundrum: Had the statute of limitation run out in August 1989, five years after Kemper paid the last installment of the settlement money to Mitch? Or had the clock not started ticking because the fraud scheme continued as long as Phil led a double life?

"The U.S. Attorney at Seattle decided in early 1993 not to explore any further mail fraud prosecution," explains Jim Bordenet, U.S. postal inspector and public information officer of the Seattle Division, "because they determined that the statute of limitations had indeed run out."

While the court docket didn't include a mail fraud arrest or conviction, postal inspectors made substantive contributions to the investigation.

"Only an arcane vagary of the law protected Champagne from standing before the bar of justice on a postal violation," comments Bordenet, "perhaps the only bar that Phillip wasn't interested in visiting."

From behind bars at Spokane's Geiger Correction Center, Phil, via the United States Postal Service, sent Mitch Champagne an "I know I owe you an explanation, so here goes" letter.

"When I fell overboard I somehow survived. I don't know how. I remember nothing for three or four days...I hope one day to go into detail in person if you are speaking to me. According to the paper they say there was a $1.5 million fraud. I knew of some insurance, but nothing like that...I hope I have not caused you so much hell that you will wish I was dead. I love you."

He also wrote Gary Penar a combination thank you and entreaty for assistance letter.

"Without your expertise, I know I would have received a more severe sentence," acknowledged Champagne. "Knowing you were on my side gave me hope and kept me sane during the darkest hour of my life."

The hours were still pretty dim. Phil begged Penar to convince prison caseworker Ray Garcia that Phil was not Ronald Kollister, an identification error which continued to plague him. Despite confirmation from the United States government that Phil was not Ron, the judge took Kollister's arrest record into consideration when sentencing Champagne.

"To compound the problem and make matters worse, they are certain that I am a drug user because of the presentence investigation report," wrote Phil from prison. "Is there any way that you can possibly make him understand the report is in error?"

In light of Phil Champagne's history of fabricated names and bogus identification, the closing request resonated with irony: "I very much appreciate any help you can give me in setting the record straight as to my true identity."

Unlike elder brother Mitch, little brother John Robin never received mail from Phil.

"My first reaction, when it was confirmed that Phil was alive, was to go see him," says John, "but I didn't know if he wanted to see me. After all, in all those years, and even after he was discovered, he didn't call me or write me. I thought—and I know this sounds crazy—I thought that maybe he was mad at me for not saving his life when he fell off the boat. I got the name of the place where they had him from Mitch, then I called and asked what I had to do to come visit him. They said he would have to put me on the visitor's list. I asked if they would see if he would do that."

Phil put John on the list.

"I figured then that he really did want to see me, so I went to Geiger, walked through the little turnstile, and there was Phil looking just like himself, and he looked pretty good."

There was no question as to whether John would hug him or slug him.

"I hugged him and held on a long, long time."

Daughter Renee and her husband, Steve Harold, also went on pilgrimage to Geiger. For the first time in more than ten years, for the first time since his watery demise, Renee gazed upon the face of her beloved father. Everyone cried.

Kathy, Curtis, and Phil Jr., did not ask to be put on the list.

"In time I hope they will come around," says Phil. "It is hard for me, too. I am the same man who raised them from childhood, but in some ways I'm not the same man they knew."

John Robin immediately noticed alterations in Phil's character and demeanor.

"It was hard talking to him because I could feel the influence living in prison was having on his mind. Some parts of him were the same as before; other parts were different. His faith in himself and his confidence were almost completely eroded. He was always the kind of person who could pretty much do whatever he decided to do. If he didn't know how to do something, he would learn how to do it. He has an extremely good mind and a great deal of perseverance. He can learn how to do anything he needs to do. It used to be that he used that talent to make money."

He used that talent to make money in an Idaho shed.

"Phil was always the eternal optimist," asserts Don Robertson. "He always believed that the next project was the one that was going to really make him money. Phil has a lot of talent, and I know he wants to make something of his life."

So did Montel Williams.

"Who is Montel Williams?" asked Phil as he went through his mail at Geiger.

Montel Williams, a former military man who now makes his living as a television talk show host, wanted to base an episode of his program around Phil Champagne. He thought it was an incredible story worthy of extensive television coverage. Williams wanted Phil, wanted an exclusive, and wanted it for free.

Inside Edition and *A Current Affair* pursued Phil, Barb, Phil's kids, Lyle Workman, Tim Ohms, Henry Kantor, and Peter Richter.

"Yumpin' Yesus," chuckled Phil, "I think I need an agent."

What he really needed was to make peace with himself, his family, and Barbara Ellen LeHew Yokum Fraley Stegeman Champagne. Both Phil and Barb were locked up in the same facility.

"We didn't get much time together, and none of it alone," says Barb, "and even though we were married, I didn't know how much of what he said to me about anything was true. After all, I didn't know he had an ex-wife and kids until I read it in the paper."

Phil could top that.

"I didn't know I was dead until I read it in the paper. All things considered, I took it rather well."

Epilogue

As subjects, we all live in suspense, from day to day, from hour to hour; in other words, we are the hero of our own story. We cannot believe that it is finished, that we are "finished," even though we may be so; we expect another chapter, another installment, tomorrow or next week.

—*Mary McCarthy*
On the Contrary

Barb saw freedom earlier than Phil. Released from Geiger, she faced the toughest time of her life.

"No matter how hard things had been in the past, the situation after I was released was the roughest of all," confirms Barb. "Our living conditions were poor, I was poorer, and Phil was still at Geiger."

On February 22, 1994, Phillip Wendell Champagne was a free man. To celebrate, he and Barb drove to Portland for a good buddy reunion with Ed Grass, Don Robertson, and John Robin. A splendid time was had by all. Mitch, still being hounded by the relentless Peter Richter, did not join his brothers for a backslapping evening of camaraderie and vodka.

"I am happy to inform you that Federal Kemper has dismissed their suit against my client, Mr. Mitch Champagne," announced a jubilant Henry Kantor in September 1994. "I am not at liberty to reveal the details of the settlement, but I can tell you that an amicable agreement has been reached; the suit has been dismissed."

Kantor's opponent, Peter Richter, was equally pleased to have the strange case of Phil Champagne finally resolved.

"I spent twelve years on that one," laughs Richter, "and now I'm on to a new one. Besides, I think Federal Kemper was getting tired of the whole thing anyway."

Life goes on in fair imitation of normalcy. Barb works in a restaurant; Phil picks up small jobs here and there and considers going on those television talk shows after all. Hollywood toys with some movie ideas, but you never know. Few folks outside show business feel comfortable hiring a high-profile felon.

"If you can't trust a man convicted of bank fraud and counterfeiting," jokes the former Harold Stegeman, "who can you trust?"

Richard Fraley, Barb's first husband, drove from Shelton's Washington Correction Center across the state and over the border into Idaho for the single purpose of making amends.

"I wanted to apologize for not being a better husband and father," admits Richard. "Maybe things would have been different for Barb and the kids if I had been there for them more. I wish Barb and Phil all the best. I know it is not going to be easy."

In a comfortable split-level house on a corner lot in a quiet suburb, Barb's grandchildren were playing on backyard swings, sucking popsicles, and crawling all over Phil Champagne. His growls elicited giggles, much as did those of Marlon Brando in *The Godfather*'s final scenes.

Sitting at the kitchen table eating cookies and swapping stories, it is difficult to envision this delightful man in his midsixties crawling through the mud on his belly to retrieve bogus bills from a Ritzville phone booth, running from Cancun assassins, or skydiving into a drug lord's lair to liberate a banker's box of illicit loot.

"Alias Mike lives somewhere in Oregon, obscure and silent, hoping no one shows up looking for him or asking questions," explains Phil. "If they do, he'll deny everything. He kinda wishes I had kept my mouth shut about all that stuff. We don't talk since the counterfeiting business, and I haven't seen him since before Barb and I left Shelton. When I got arrested, that was the last straw as far as being close friends went. He saved my life, and when he gave it back to me, I screwed it up."

Phil examines his empty glass.

"I called Mitch the other day and asked him if he was still mad at me. I never wanted to cause him problems, and I wondered if he still felt that his problems were all my fault."

Champagne rearranges a few cookie crumbs on the table.

"There wasn't much said, except that I should just let it go, that he wasn't mad anymore, but..." Champagne shrugs, looks wistfully out the window, and shifts the subject as he gets up from the table to get fresh ice for another round of soft drinks.

"Years ago Joanne, the kids, and I were visiting her mother, Florence LeGate. Someone is always supposed to take pictures when families get together, so I was taking pictures. I wanted Renee to sit on a ladder while I took her snapshot. I couldn't get her to smile. I kept telling her to smile, but the sun was in her eyes. I got so irked at her for not smiling that I raised my voice, and the poor little girl started to cry. God, I felt like such a stupid ass making my kid cry just to take her picture."

Champagne returns to the table, glass and cookie in hand. He sits down, still talking about his kids as if they were not adults who, for the most part, want little or nothing to do with him.

"My son, Curtis, was born with what they call a lazy eye. He had to have them operated on when he was about four. His mother didn't get into these things, so I had to take him to the doctor and the hospital and decide if he needed the operation. They operated on his eyes, doing something to the muscles."

Champagne stops, laughs self-consciously, and dabs at his own eyes with a convenience store napkin.

"He was in his bed when I got there and his eyes were bandaged but one of the bandages had come loose. I got mad and gave the nurse hell. The whole time Curtis had been lying there, waiting, and he couldn't see. And then I heard a little voice say, 'Daddy? Is that you?'"

As if his postdeath adventures and Curtis's eye operation were inseparable events, Phil Champagne finishes the story.

"I had always thought I would come back to life sooner or later, although I couldn't see how it would happen. Then again, were it not for the counterfeiting, I could have lived out my life as Harold Stegeman and gone to my grave without anyone ever knowing I had once been Phil Champagne."

Phil's critical thinking abilities have not changed much since second grade. And, for the record, he is not sorry that he ran away from home.

"Had I not gone for it when I had the chance, I never would have experienced a decade of adventure, romance, danger, wealth, and what they call living under the shadow of the sword, and I never would have met Barb. Through everything, she loved me. She still loves me, and that's worth more than all the real money and fake money put together."

Lyle Workman has retired from the Secret Service. His big adventure is watching his son play baseball for Pepperdine University.

Assistant U.S. Prosecutor Timothy Ohms has matured into a respected professional who no longer frets about his future while sipping holiday eggnog.

The former site of Barb's Country Kitchen and Stegey's Blue Room is, at last report, vacant and available.

Extensive remodeling has beautified Perkins Restaurant in Ritzville, Washington. Linda Bright is still there serving up breakfasts and making change at the cash register. No hundreds, please.